THE FALEN DISTINGUISHED JUDGE:
The Constitutional Laws Fundamentalist

Justice Bullen Panchol Awal Alier

By

Majok Wutchok

BP
Bor Publishers

Bor Publishers © 2020.

 A catalogue record for this work is available from the National Library of Australia

Copyright © 2020 - Majok Wutchok

All rights reserved. No part of this guide may be reproduced in any form without permission in writing from the publisher except in the case of brief quotations embodied in critical articles or reviews.

Legal & Disclaimer

The information contained in this book and its contents is not designed to replace or take the place of any form of professional advice; and is not meant to replace the need for independent, legal or other professional advice or services, as may be required. The content and information in this book have been provided for educational and entertainment purposes only.

The content and information contained in this book has been compiled from sources deemed reliable, and it is accurate to the best of the Author's knowledge, information and belief. However, the Author cannot guarantee its accuracy and validity and cannot be held liable for any errors and/or omissions. Further, changes are periodically made to this book as and when needed. Where appropriate and/or necessary, you must consult a professional (including but not limited to your attorney or other professional advisor) before using any of the suggested information in this book.

Bor Publishers,
Perth, Western Australia
Phone: 08 9439 4704
Email: admin@borpublishers.com
Web: www.borpublishers.com
ABN: 45 867 024 044
ISBN: 978-0-6482848-7-1

DEDICATION

This book is dedicated to South Sudan's critical judge, Late Justice Bullen Panchol Awal Alier.

CONTENTS

Acknowledgments 1

Preface 3

Chapter 1

Childhood- Growing Up Amidst Independence And Civil Wars 9

Chapter 2

Pursuit Of Passion- Studying Law. 20

Chapter 3

Graduation And What's Next? 28

Chapter 4

South Sudan's Independence & The Aftermath: The Judicial Challenges And Changes. 35

Chapter 5

Getting Personal: Justice Bullen Panchol As A Family Man Till His Final Moments. 78

Chapter 6

Another Loss For The Panchols: Tragic Passing Of Martin Panchol Awal (Alier-Marto). 86

Book/ Phase 2 – Judge Bullen Panchol's Ambition, Hard Work And Legacy.

Chapter 7

Full Autonomy Of The Judiciary: Building The Ideal Legal System Of South Sudan. 100

Chapter 8

Better Life For The Girl Child: Education Empowerment And Fight Against Underage Marriage. 104

Chapter 9

Setting Up Tough Preventive Measures Against The Abduction Of Children By Cattle Rustlers In Jonglei State. 108

Chapter 10

Controlled Nomadic Ranging: Introducing Prohibitive Laws To Castle Rustlers. 115

Chapter 11

Bring Law And Order To The Grassroots: **Rural Villages.** 119

Conclusion **134**

Gallery **135**

ACKNOWLEDGMENTS

While Justice Bullen Panchol Awal Alier's family were going through brutal double tragedies that took Judge Bullen and his older son Martin Alier. I was aware of the need to ensure family cohesiveness and energy to convey an encouraging, motivated and positive attitude toward the devastating family members around the globe that had heard bad news befallen. In order to provide high levels of Judge Bullen's family supports, long days were often required for many people to stay around with Uncle Bullen Panchol's children specially in Juba, Uganda, Kenya and Canada. Those family comforters were successfully motivating Judge Bullen's children to mitigates emotional lost and difficulties accepting by effectively managing concerns, maintaining motivation levels, and providing appropriate future advices. It's with great acknowledgement to mention those who have sacrifices their times, moral supports, financial supports, spiritual supports, emotional supports, that Judge Bullen Panchol and his son are sincerely proud of your work. Wholeheartedly, my acknowledgement and appreciation goes to general citizen of Jonglei State, Pan Baidit, Angakuei people, Palek people (Pan Tiir Angok), Kongor people, Judge Bullen's best friends, his sons Eng. Deng Diar Diing, Samuel Ayuen Bullen Panchol, Tiir Bullen Panchol, Jooh Bullen Panchol, Kut Bullen Panchol, (his daughters)

Suzy Bullen Panchol, Marina Bullen Panchol, Apiu Bullen Panchol, Asara Bullen Panchol, Avena Diing Bullen Panchol, Nyiel-thi Bullen Panchol, Mary Bullen Panchol, Deng Ayor Awal, Abit Ayor Awal, Bul Ayen Awal, Gaar Majak Awal, Ayor Denbion Alier and his sons, Manyola Ajak, Ajakthi Dengbion Alier, Panchol Alier, Alakiir Ayor Awal, Aluet Ayen Awal, Mongok Gai Mangok, Malith Ayiu Aluong, Gaar Gai Alier, Ajakdit Dengbion Alier, Mach Ayen Awal, Achol Awal Alier, Ayor Awal Alier, Dr. Peter Biar Ajak (Biar Ayor Awal), Dr. Awar Ayuen Awar, Dr. Angok Kuol Tiir, Dr. Akim Kuol Tiir, Amb. Maluk Mach Tiir, Abenydit Kuol Tiir, Ayen Kuol Tiir, Leek Kuol Tiir, Dr. Mayom Kuoirot, Ateny Thiong Ajak, and some great South Sudan government officials, I say, thank you. Atong Ayen Awal in Canada and I, were responsible for the technical architecture, implementation and managing the operations of the family communication and coordination, I say, thank you Atong Ayen. Special gratitude and appreciation goes to my wife Eunice Ndungu and our children for allowing me to spend sleepless night on a computer writing everyday to compiled and write notes.

This support team was very diverse, in areas such as, family make-up, age, health status, educational background, experience and skill level. Judge Bullen Panchol and Martin Alier are proud of you all. Thank you for kind support during difficult time.

PREFACE

In the dark evening of May 13th, 2020, right in the onset of the world newest pandemic COVID-19, the death and the passing of one of South Sudan's most honourable Justice and distinguished judge was announced by medical expert in consultation with his family in Juba, South Sudan. South Sudan has suffered a huge loss to its Judiciary system and legal fraternity. Justice Bullen Panchol Awal Alier drew his last breathe within the hour of 8:30 PM in the evening, Juba local time. According to medical report released after his passing, late Judge suffered and succumbed to HEART ATTACK.

South Sudan has lost a keen fighter of justice, a beacon of hope, truth, and transparency in the judicial system to the snares of a short illness. Even though the cause of his passing or nature of sickness was later reported to be heart attack. However, there has been a hint that the Late judge did suffered major a symptom-like shortness of breath, a symptom of the deadly heart attack. South Sudan was in a state of mourning as one of the founding fathers of South Sudan's democracy and the judiciary system is no more. Justice Bullen Panchol Awal Alier, the first-ever South Sudanese to be a second high ranked of Sudanese Constitutional Court has ascended into the heaven to be one of South Sudan's impactful ancestors.

During his lifetime, Justice Bullen Panchol was not only an active advocate of some sort, he was as well as a man of many hats, although most certainly wigs and robes. He was more dedicated to the struggle of fairness in the judicial system of the South Sudanese people. He has fought against nepotism, corruption, bribery, and other moral and political decadence slowly eating up the democracy and justice system of South Sudan. Relentless and in the fore-front of exemplary works that bring South Sudan the deserved rights and transparency that is cherished in the ideal democratic society. An epitome of optimism and a firm believer of all citizens of South Sudan living together in harmony and with equal opportunities. One could easily see that the above ideal was all he hoped, fought, and lived to achieve and also died trying to achieve.

Right before he resigned in September 2018 in South Sudan's Judiciary system, Justice Bullen played a pivotal role in the constitutional court for the position of supreme judge of the then constitutional court in Khartoum, having been appointed by the late Dr. John Garang de Mabior (the then Sudanese Vice President and President of the Government of Southern Sudan 2005) for 6 years i.e. 2005 – 2011. Then, in September of year 2011, Justice Bullen Panchol Awal Alier was appointed as a judge to South Sudan Supreme court by the current South Sudanese President, Salva Kiir Mayardit. He was confirmed alongside other three judges by South Sudan legislative assembly. Right before he resumed the position of a Judge in South Sudan's SPLA/SPLM Supreme Court, Justice Bullen was a seasoned soldier in his prime and retired in 2018 with the noble rank of Major General. Being the first South Sudanese to be second high ranked judge of Sudanese constitutional court after 21 years of divisional war between the Northern and Southern Sudan was no small achievement. Right after his retirement at SPLA, Justice Bullen was a fine man with an incredible work ethic. As the saying goes, a musician never stops making music only until he no longer has music in him. Justice Awal retired into private practices where he established his own private law firm and founded Alier Gaar Law firm which had offices in Juba and Bor Town.

While in the Justice System, he was faced with the glaring truth about the cankerworm i.e. Corruption eating deep and wreaking havoc in the political, democratic, and humanitarian part of the country. Justice Bullen was among the rather few intellectuals and outliers of South Sudan. He was highly respected and acknowledged for his rather strict and thorough ruling and impeccable statement of judgment. Without having a one-on-one sitting with high profile, you could see clearly his passion and vision for the country was to see nationalism and patriotism in leadership. He was an advocate of fairness, transparency and a South Sudan free from violence. Also, his austere conduct and code for transparency calibre made him an easy target to being hated and other controversial deeds to make him compromise on his ideals.

Most government officials who wanted to loot the country's financial system and land grabbing see Justice Bullen as a huge threat to their scheme and corruption. As a result of the rotten and neck-deep corruption, he resigned from judiciary in 2018. While at it, Justice Bullen outrightly highlighted some of the problems causing the instability of the government and judicial system of South Sudan. He explicitly addressed how it has impacted the proper function of the democratic system in order for it to function as an exemplary judicial service provider. As a scholar and a lover of youth and education, any youth who get to have a meeting, be it long or short period with the judge, leaves with getting full with motivation, the zeal to want to attain a better position in life, and most importantly impacting your country in a positive way. Although welcoming and approachable, Justice Bullen is strict and thorough when it comes to law and other judicial matter pertaining to his country. You could see, hear his affinity for law and order, his passion for violent free South Sudan, and as an academic giant, he speaks with eloquence, pride, and utmost confidence. In his quest to reform South Sudan and also make South Sudan a prime example of the best judicial system in Africa as a whole. Sadly, that is not the case of present South Sudan as its justice system is punctuated with different types of problems ranging from illegal possession of firearms, poverty, illiteracy, injustice, mismanagement, murder cases, robbery, abused of power etc.

As should be within his rights, he should be laid to rest alongside other recognised comrades and martyrs of the state. However, due to his transparency, straightforwardness and a firm stance against corruption, injustice, weak accountability, inability to lead, political instability and security brutality, he was denied the honour of being buried amongst heroes of South Sudan. This purported decline was made without any logical explanations to back it up from nation's top leadership on who is martyr or who is holy to be call martyr in South Sudan? After what seems to be a memorable, selfless, active, and zealous 70 years of existence, Justice Bullen Panchol was temporally put to rest in his Juba home, a new resident built for him by his daughters and sons. The family is planning building Justice Bullen Panchol's memorial park in his homeland Bor, Jonglei State where his remains of his body will be exhumed and transported to Bor, Jonglei State for final resting in near future.

This is a book that covers the ups-and down roller-coaster life as well as an intense personality of an avid law maker who lived through military regime, the war between the North and South Sudan, and the democratic phase before retiring into private law practices. He was a nation diehard critical judge and was nicknamed by public as "No NONESENSE JUDGE", due to his tough ruling stand.

In addition, this book is also about hope and reawakening the belief of a better South Sudan free from injustice, corruption, poverty, imposition of rule of law in rural villages, laws on cattle rustlings, child abductions laws, and nepotism. If not anything, this book hopes to re-instil the spirit of a freedom fighter for a just cause, in the same way justice Bullen Panchol would have or even better. For Justice Bullen Panchol Awal Alier, the ascension to heaven of a perfect judicial judge without any blemish starts with the willingness to be selfless, putting one's country first, and making South Sudan constitution and Judicial system be one other African country try to emulate.

Majok Wutchok
Perth, Western Australia
October 2020.

Other Books authored and published by Majok Wutchok.

Unimaginatively Western World! (What makes immigrants parents struggle raising their children in western world), 2018.

Introduction to County Public Health Strategic Plan (County Level, South Sudan). Plan Guideline book, 2018.

Socioeconomic Disadvantage and Poverty in Polygyny African Families, 2018.

"Justice Bullen Panchol Awal:

South Sudan has lost one of its refined and seasoned lawyers, Justice Bullen Panchol, member of the Supreme Court of South Sudan. I came to know Justice Panchol when Dr John Garang appointed us in 1991 to the legal and constitutional committee to draft and review basic laws for the New Sudan to be presented to the SPLM National Convention in 1994. The committee was chaired by Commander Ayuen Alier (the current Director of the DDR Commission) and I was the only economist on the committee. During our deliberations over various laws, Justice Panchol exhibited rare traits of professionalism, integrity, humility and nobility. We became friends since then and I worked closely with him when he was a member of national constitutional court in Khartoum, a duty that he performed with distinction. One of his closest friends remembered him as one of the few elders who would like to be associated with his mother, as he would always introduce himself in social gatherings as Panchol Abeny. Justice Panchol would be remembered as freedom fighter, martyr and one of the founders of legal system for South Sudan. My condolences to his family and relatives. May Almighty God Rest His Soul in Eternal Peace."

Dr. Luka Biong

CHAPTER ONE

CHILDHOOD - GROWING UP AMIDST INDEPENDENCE AND CIVIL WARS

South Sudan is divided into three historic provinces i.e. the contemporary regions of Bahr el Ghazal (Northwest), Equatoria (Southern), and Greater Upper Nile (Northeast). Then, South Sudan was politically divided into 10 states, three administrative areas and these states were further divided into 86 Southern Sudan counties. These 10 states are namely Central Equatoria State, Eastern Equatoria State, Jonglei State, Lakes State, Northern Bahr el Ghazal state, Unity state, Upper Nile state, Warrap state, Western Bahr el Ghazal state, and Western Equatoria State. The Administrative Areas are Ruweng, Abyei and Greater Pibor. However, by population and landmass area, Jonglei state is the largest state in South Sudan. According to the 2008 census, Jonglei state as of 2010 had approximately more than 1.4 million people with a landmass area of approximately 123,000km2. The capital of Jonglei state is Bor, while other important towns in Jonglei includes: Ayod, Boma, Akobo, Duk, Fangak, Pochalla, Panyangor and Waat. Bor, the capital city of Jonglei was the birthplace of Justice Bullen. Judge Bullen Panchol Awal Alier was born on 8th April 1950 in Baidit Payam, Bor County, Jonglei State. The late Justice's father Awal Alier Gaar Jooh was a native of the Angakuei clan, Leek Ajak section. Alier Gaar descendants are among the largest families among Bor people, the two sons are Awal Alier Gaar, Deng-bion Alier Gaar and daughters are Nyariak Alier Gaar and Nyayuon Alier Gaar, all has traces everywhere within Bor. It was Justice Bullen Panchol Awal holding education prestige in towns with younger Alier Gaar's decendents, while his cousin Ayor Deng-bion Alier holding prestige traditions and cattle wealth of Alier Gaar's huge family in the village. The two duos of Alier Gaar's family were bonding large families in greater spirit and living in greater harmony.

The Angakuei community is the largest clan in Bor, following of other communities such as Kongor, Hol Padiet, Palek, and Ayual communities of Greater Bor, Jonglei State. Angakuei is also the clan of the first vice president of the former Sudan and the president of the High Executive Council of Southern Sudan Honourable Abel Alier Wal Kuai Kut.

Palek clan, Anyidi community in Jonglei state South Sudan famously known for its highly competitive with people of great geek calibre, cattle wealth, agricultural farming and fish farming strengths. The Palek clan or Anyidi community is headquartered in Anyidi town courtship of Bor County with its proximity to the Nile River and bordering notorious tribe, the Murle. Justice Bullen Panchol's mother Abeny Tiir Angok was a native of the Palek clan, Kuchdok section. The Tiir Angok family is one of highly well-structured families in Bor, Jonglei State, engulfed enormously enough with high profile towering figures and highly well-educated people. Justice Bullen Panchol's maternal uncles and aunties are most distinguished people and highly achievers where young and old of Tiir Angok descendant is a graduate from university. More importantly, in most high profiles meetings Justice Bullen Panchol attended, he would introduce himself as "Justice Panchol Abeny Tiir", showing sense of attachment and belonging he had towards his maternal family, his passion for love and unity is what is seen with descendants of Tiir Angok huge families. He grew up in his early years of high school with his maternal uncle's children where he embraced his great affection toward people. People glanced at Tiir Angok family with sense of pride, people talked of Dr. Angok Kuol Tiir, Dr. Akim Kuol Tiir, (Upcoming

Tiir young medical doctors: Dr. Abeny Akim Kuol Tiir and Dr. Thiong Angok Kuol Tiir), Dr. Abeny Maluk Mach Tiir, Eng. Yuot Abeny Kucha Tiir, Social Work Advocate Ayen Kuol Tiir, Eng. Leek Kuol Tiir, Ambassador Maluk Mach Tiir, Ambassador Dr. Tony Aluel Kuol Tiir, Eng. Biem Angok Kuol Tiir, Eng. Tiir Angok Kuol Tiir, Naturalist Jok Tiir Kuol Tiir and many more successful of Tiir Angok's descendants I haven't mentioned here.

Even though we cannot say for certain when Justice Bullen's parent got married, the couple gave birth to a baby-bouncing boy Bullen Panchol in the year 1950 in Baidit, Bor, Jonglei South Sudan. During his time of birth, Sudan was still colonized by the British under the British-Egyptian rule. As of then, South Sudan was as part of the Anglo-Egyptian Sudan. On the 1st of January 1956, the Republic of Sudan gain its independence with zero conflict. However, while at its Sudan inherited some condominiums. Sudan gained independence without the rival political parties. Each party agreed on the content and form of a permanent constitution. Rather, the Constituent Assembly embraced a document known as the Transitional Commission. This document replaced the governor-general as the Head of state with a five-member Supreme Commission that was elected by a law parliament that consist of an indirectly elected Senate and also a famously elected House of Representatives. The 1956 Transitional Constitution also apportioned executive power to the prime minister nominated by the House of Representatives which was confirmed in office by the Supreme Commission.

The Long Road to Independence.

Anyone would be right to categorize South Sudan as one of the newest nations in history. Going by history, South Sudan was once part of the Republic of Sudan, the country to its north. The irreconcilable conflicts between South Sudan and Sudan of today are often implied through their roots in history. Both nations while still together experienced centuries of slave-raiding and exploitation by the "Arab" north against the "African" south in which what ensued was Britain and Egypt's imperial meddling. According to history, the Arab tribes first arrived in Sudan from Upper Egypt, and across the Red Sea during the Middle Ages. Then, the colonial occupation started in the 19th century. Nevertheless, we cannot categorically explain Sudan's recent conflicts from any perspective or in simple terms. Even though the colour of the skin, religion, colonialism, and exploitation played a major role in the crises, none of the aforementioned factors can give a better or detailed explanation into the conflict situation.

Starting with the imperialist intervention, the following is a brief timeline or phases that led to the phase of the independence of the Republic of Sudan. In 1820, Egypt conquered the northern parts of Sudan and subjecting most indigenes into slaves and exploiting its natural resources. This led to the development of ivory and slave trades in Sudan. This nightmare continued until 1880 when Nationalists led by Muhammad Ahmad Al Mahdi revolts by forming an opposition to the Egyptian and British rule. As of then, Egypt was under the authority of British occupation). The Egyptians and the British were defeated in 1885 and Al Mahdi set up a theocracy government in Khartoum. However, the victory was short-lived as the British regained control of Sudan with military campaigns in 1890, which was led by Lord Kitchener. In the year 1899, Britain and Egypt reached a consensual joint government of Sudan. This continued very roughly and in 1930, the British Civil Secretary in Khartoum announced the "Southern Policy" officially declaring what had always been in practice i.e. the North and South, as a result of their religious and cultural differences, hence they were governed as two separate regions. In 1946, with Egypt out of the governing bodies, Britain and Khartoum brusquely decide to merge north and south regions of Sudan into a single administrative region. Arabic was chosen as the official language of administration in the south where northerners are also given administrative positions to hold as well. This continued until the republic of Sudan worked its way to independence with zero conflict as a single unified nation on the 1st of January 1956. Before the open declaration of independence from Anglo-Egyptian rule, in 1955 while anticipating independence and dreading domination by the northern region, the southern insurgents staged a rebellion in Torit town. These early revolutionaries develop a large secessionist movement in the south, known as the Anyanya Movement. The Anyanya movement later had it bad with several internal factionalism as well as instability, for instance, the SPLA and how they handled the second civil war in Sudan.

In 1955, the Anyanya One took arms against the government in Khartoum. This led to the beginning of the first civil war which began in January 1955. A year before Sudan gained its independence from the British in 1956. The Lt- Joseph Lagu, was the leader of the Anyanya rebels at that time. Mr. Joseph Lagu mobilized men of South Sudan in the small town of Torit and declared war against the government of Sudan. In 1956, the British left the government leaving the Arabs to take over the government, hence, exercising their inhumane acts against the people of South Sudan as well as other indigenous groups within Sudan.

The Anyanya rebels were a small faction with zero support from any international community. They were guerrilla warfare with limited guns and ammunition as well. However, they struggled for representation as well as more regional autonomy in South Sudan. The war continued for 17 years, where the Organization of African Union (O.A.U) currently known as African Union (AU) negotiated the peace dialogue between the rebels and Sudan government in 1972. The peace deal was signed in Ethiopia which is known as the Addis Ababa Agreement.

After the agreements were signed, the Anyanya rebels left the bush and returned to Sudan with their rebel leader Mr. Joseph Lagu. Well ahead, the rebels were disarmed and recruited into the national army of Sudan. The agreement which was signed in 1972 considered South Sudan as regional autonomy. The transitional government was formed between the rebels in South Sudan and the government in North Sudan. In the space of five years, the people of South Sudan were ready to fully exercise their referendum that would guarantee their self-determination.

Five years later, the Arab led government sullied the peace agreement by considered peace regarded as illegitimate or mere sheets of paper. According to the Arab's perspective at the time, the agreement was a gimmick to disarm the rebels. Moreover, the agreement was not a religious act. During that time, the former President of Sudan Col- Jaafar Muhammad Al-Nimeiry uttered a blind blather statement against the peace protocols. In his own words, "This peace agreement is just a piece of paper; it is neither the Quran nor the Bible". Due to the fact of how religiously-inclined the Arabs are, they place more importance on piety resources, hence believe anything that comes from God. Also, it was obvious that the Addis Ababa Agreement was negotiated by men not their reverenced God. In that sense, the peace agreement was dishonoured in the name of religion because it was in the Arabs' favour.

In Sudan, the peace protocols were regarded as illegitimate. The agreement was dishonoured by the regime simply because they could use military force against the people of South Sudan. At gunpoint, the Addis Ababa agreement was stolen from the South Sudanese people and the new phase of brutality against natives started across South Sudan and North Sudan as well. It was the beginning of the Dark Age in Sudan and because of that, the peace agreements were demolished at the gunpoint. Since then, people of South Sudan were intimidated and subjected to countless massacres on regular basis by the brutal regime.

The referendum was suspended, and Islamic laws were introduced against the people of South Sudan. With such conditions, the people of South Sudan became slaves again for many years. The African natives in Sudan became victims of torture, oppression, and prosecution of people without trials. Women, children, old people were victims of rapes, violations, and extreme genocides. There are some unrecorded massacres that occurred in Sudan without enough world attention due to a lack of media coverage.

*   *   *

Judge Bullen Panchol's Education Journey Amid Wars

Growing up as a child in the era of gaining independence and instigations of civil war is not what a regular child should experience. Justice Bullen Panchol Awal has been one of the few who cut themselves out at the early age of their education and life as intelligent, objective, and bold. This is one quality that won him foes and friends alike. This same quality remained his brand throughout his public service. One would not be wrong to say that his hard experiences as a little boy in the bush during the liberation struggle made him a fearless activist and a zealous South Sudan citizen who is up for fairness and justice. Since his childhood, he has always felt and sided with the liberators especially when they have been elbowed out by swindlers of their hard-won Freedom.

Even in the midst of the brooding dystopia in the republic of Sudan then, Justice Bullen was enrolled in a school in a nearby village Baidit Bush School from 1957 to 1959. Then, he proceeds in his education and was enrolled in Malek Elementary school in Bor from 1960 to 1962. He graduated elementary school and enrolled into Obel Junior Secondary school, during this time particularly 1962, the civil war led by Anyanya One, a southern separatist, who began the movement with the northern region was literally very active. Even though the war has not blown over the entire nation, those were difficult times, making education a serious need but difficult to achieve. In spite of the difficulties encountered, Bullen Panchol continued his education as he graduated to enrol in Rumbek Senior Secondary school in 1966 – 1968.

Upon completion of his elementary and secondary education, Bullen Panchol decided to study law at the University of Khartoum. In 1969, a new policy that outlines the autonomy of Southern Sudan was formed. A group of communists and socialists in the Sudanese military offices led by Colonel Jaafar Muhammad Numeiri seized power. Panchol got admitted into the University of Khartoum in 1970 amid boiling insurgency in the country, he later earned his honours degree LLB in August 1975. During the course of his study, he was already a trained child soldier from Anyanya One Movement. However, in the 1970s in Sudan, the country was a ticking time bomb, amidst all the chaos, the "liquid wealth" was discovered in some parts of Sudan. During the 1970s, as Sudan gains legitimacy, other Western countries began to supply the government with arms.

The US sold Sudan a lot of arms hoping to counter the Soviet support of Marxist Ethiopians as well as Libyans. In 1972, all rebel groups under the control of the Southern Sudan Liberation Movement (SSLM) gather to negotiate a peace agreement with the Sudanese government. The agreement which is referred to as the Addis Ababa Agreement was signed by the government, granting the southern region of Sudan considerable autonomy and a substantial share of natural resources. This was followed by a ten-year hiatus in the conflict. In 1978, Chevron discovered large oil fields in the Upper Nile, Unity State in southern Sudan, and Southern Kordofan regions.

Shortly after this discovery, further intensive exploration was carried out, oil was discovered throughout Southern Sudan. In 1980, Khartoum attempts to redraw boundaries of Southern Sudan, thereby transferring oilfield to the north. As expected, this attempt experienced a fatal failure, Khartoum started taking up territories by force, one of which included Muglad Basin. The Muglad Basin is simply an area closer to the north-south border which was claimed by Khartoum and renamed 'Wahda', the Arabic word for "Unity".

After his graduation from the University of Khartoum with LLB honours in Law, Bullen later enrolled in Law School and passed his bar exams. In the year 1975, after graduating with an honorary degree in Law, he plunged into the law profession starting out as a legal assistant in the Republic of Sudan before he got swayed into the military. Bullen Panchol was among the first from his batch deployed to the Judiciary where he served till 1984. He began working in a number of Law related niches in Sudan and also the far South. He continued in the judiciary until he resigned as a presiding judge in Yambio to join the Sudan People's Liberation Movement in 1984. In 1985, he graduated in Bonga with Zalzal Division as captain and judicial personnel after his resignation.

During the time of the civil war, the urban border dramatically built around the government military base, where its inhabitants found themselves under siege between two antagonistic '*hakumas*' i.e. the rebel government in the bush as well as the government in town. Both the town and bush were abstruse moral spaces, and the chiefs as well as their communities who wrestled with how to stay safe and gain protection during the first and second civil war. Each community that had been formed by the late-colonial era in the vicinity of the two times was often divided and scattered to different areas.

While serving as a second-class judge in the Sudan judiciary, he was promoted to the acting mainstream province judge in 1984 in the former Western Equatoria before joining his kinsmen in the liberation struggle. After joining SPLA/SPLM military training in Ethiopia, he was later dispatched to the field in South Sudan with the Zalzal Battalion serving several regions in South Sudan. While still in the bush fighting for the liberation of his country, Justice Bullen Panchol doubled as a soldier and a head of judicial court in the bush. In the words of the tough and justice-seeking lawyer "I handled civil and criminal cases in the SPLA controlled areas, we were running the court in bushes". The mastery of his legal practices and judicial ruling gave no room for doubt. In 1994, Justice Bullen Panchol was appointed Justice to the Constitutional Court when the military was separated at the Chukudum Convention.

He continued serving in the aforementioned portfolio and in this position until the year 2000 when he was promoted and ranked to a higher military position as the alternate commander to full commander in late 2000. While still in the position of captain, Justice Pullen was arrested by the SPLA in the 1990s due to his rather admirable stance and being a fearless lawyer. This harassment segregation imprisonment was targeted to Bor political leaders with the presumption of arguments that doesn't add up onto what Dr. Garang was proposing. It's widely argues that Dr. John Garang wanted to eliminate and execute brainy Bor sons, the like of Late Justice Majier Gai who was silently murdered in prison. Justice Bullen Panchol survived from the same prison Late Justice Martin was brutally murdered in. One of the detainees he was arrested with at Kansuk said this about Justice Bullen Panchol

"When we were arrested at Kansuk, Justice Panchol was the only person who could be allowed to go and look for mangoes for us to survive. He would walk for many kilometres just to go and find food for us. We suffered during the SPLA, but Panchol remained patriotic." This is when Dr. Garang ordered all Bor intellectuals arrested and tortured.

The Fallen Distinguished Judge: The Constitutional Laws Fundamentalist

The Beginning of Second Civil War.

Under the leadership of Dr. John Garang, fighting broke out between north and South Sudan. The fight was led by the Sudanese People's Liberation Movement after the autonomy of South Sudan was ruled out by the then President Jaafar Numeiri. This led to the military seizing power in Sudan in 1989. The north-south peace deal was born in January 2005 where the North/South Comprehensive Peace Agreement brought an end to civil war.

The deal provides a permanent ceasefire, and autonomy for the southern region, as well as a democratic government in Khartoum and south Sudanese referendum on independence in a period of six years. Dr. John Garang, the former southern rebel leader was sworn in as the first Vice President to which a new Sudanese constitution that gives the south region a large degree of autonomy is signed into law. Shortly after he was appointed the first Vice President, the South Sudanese leader died in a plane crash and was succeeded by General Salva Kiir Mayardiit. Prior to the unfortunate demise of Dr. John Garang, Justice Bullen Panchol was appointed as a member of the Sudan constitutional court. Upon signing the permanent ceasefire in 2002, the preparation for governing the state, Justice Bullen Panchol took a Study leave to pursue a degree in Germany to further his education. As one of the leading delegates who negotiated certain protocols that are now referred to as Machakos Protocols, which resulted in the ceasefire of the hostilities between the North and South regions of Sudan. He obtained an LLM, Constitutional law from his alma mater Heidelberg University, Germany (2002-2003). Then, proceeded to Max Plunk Institute Germany (2003-2004) Fellowship, for Comparative Constitutional and International Law.

The Era of Fragile Peace

In November 2006, hundreds of Sudanese died fighting for Malakal – a southern town, which has been the heaviest battle ground between the northern Sudanese forces and the first rebels since the 2005 peace deal. However, tensions arose over as there was a clash between SPLM and Arab Militia over the oil-rich Abyei area along the north-south border to which a major sticking point is the 2005 peace accord. This led to north and south Sudan acceptance of the arbitration court ruling in The Hague shrinking disputed Abyei region and placing the major Heglig oil field in the north.

CHAPTER TWO
PURSUIT OF PASSION - STUDYING LAW.

Sudan, before the age of civil rights and independence, education had quite a long history with the Sudanese people. Based on historical facts and documents, the average Sudanese learned to read and write Egyptian during the reign of the Kingdom of Kush. The Kushite language was written on Meroitic script, it originated in the Sudanese city of Meroe between 700BC and 300BC. In the 13th century, regular religious classroom education *Khalawi* was introduced, it is believed to increase the spread of Islam. During this time the teaching, memorization, and interpretation of the Quran. Not only that, pupils were taught basic arithmetic and Arabic. As an estimate, the total number of Khalawi establishment was 1500, hence contributing to the literacy of approximately 60,000 pupils.

Then, during the Turkish-Egyptian rule in 1825-1885, regular schools started to appear, and the state built more schools during the British-Egyptian rule in 1898-1956. During those times, girls were at a disadvantage as there was a high percentage of out-of-school girls as compared to boys. Yet the schools in the Educational Egyptian mission significantly contributed to public education of Sudanese, the same applies to foreign Christian evangelicals establishing schools privately. This trend kickstarted in the 1950s, and since then there has been a commendable increase in education.

Since the introduction of education in Sudan, there have been several modifications in the 20th century. Education was divided into categories with four years interval each i.e. The Primary, Middle, and Secondary school. Then in the 1970s, primary education was extended to 6 years while the middle and secondary school remained 3 years, this was regulated as an education policy in 1969-1985 by General Jaafar Nimeri's administration. Referred to as the 'Salvation government', the administration of President Omar al-Bashir had the primary education extended to 8 years i.e. it merged the first and second stages together. The secondary education still had 3 years, thereby extending years of Education to 11-12 years. This is without the mandatory Khalawi or kindergarten mandated by the Sudanese Education body.

After conquering Khalifa in 1899 by Kitchener at Omdurman, Sudan was under an Anglo-Egyptian Condominium Government until it gained its independence in 1956. Although, the journey to independence from the Anglo-Egyptian Condominium government started in 1951 but transitioned into full independence in 1956. Prior to Sudan's independence, the law applicable in Sudan in personal matters since the defeat of Khalifa in 1899-1956 was Customary or Muslim law. To some certain extent, it contains reasonably few regulations issued by the government to which it does include criminal and criminal procedure codes and legislation pertaining to civil justice and procedure. Initially, the English-trained judges tried to give their verdict according to the law which both parties presumably envisioned to govern their attempts and their translations were also made to apply a couple of foreign laws. However, this did not last for long and most importantly, the judicial bench came into perspective with little justification that as it was much more difficult for a typical English lawyer to discover how to apply a foreign law than to apply the law in cases were engaged to act according to equity, a good conscience, and justice. However, for land law, the Sudanese custom has its predominant source from the Sudanese law. In the absence of prescribed basic law, the judge-made law is designed to take its place. These leaves give the court the unique position of having to administer common law rules without access to all local precedents.

In Sudan, education is categorised into regular i.e. formal education and non-regular education (Hallway, Farming, Nutrition, and Technical centres for children with special needs). A typical secondary school in Sudan covers 4 courses i.e. academic, technical, Islamic, and vocational courses. However, that of academics which covers literary and scientific aspects of education is most prevalent which covers about 97% of the total population of schools in Sudan. Higher education started in 1912 with the setting up of Omdurman Scientific Institute which is somewhat of an Islamic high school with similar operations like al-Azhar in Egypt. The emergence of universities in Sudan started when the Salvation government were in power, and Sudan had seven public universities, two private universities and some colleges and institutes as of 1989. Transitioning to the revolution of higher education mainly set the increasing admissions into higher institutes and universities hence taking out Arabic and English as a medium of instruction at universities. Following these resolutions was a pronouncement declared by the then Minister of higher education to build 19 new public universities. This resulted in the establishment of colleges and private universities. Sudan had 52 national and private colleges, 8 research centres, and 24 technical colleges.

Despite these, the illiteracy in Sudan was at an alarming rate, to which one of the major causes was the high illiteracy rate of females. In the cause of civilization and Urbanization of Sudan in the 70s, 80s, and 90s, despite the civil wars, a high rate of school dropouts was recorded as a result of insurgency and insecurities. The dystopia that occurred to Sudan after its independence led to the breeding of freedom fighters, activists, rebel groups, etc. The fight for justice where and when saws a great increase or need both on the battlefield and in the bathroom. Growing up in such an environment can influence a child's decision about life. Finding oneself amid war, corruption, and injustice gives any growing child just two choices, join the decadence or make a change. In the case of Justice Bullen Panchol, he recognised the pestilence and how its continuation will inherently disrupt the country he calls home from the inside-out. Despite all the happenings, Bullen proceeded to study law at the University of Khartoum. After his successful completion of the four-year-long academic years, he further plunged into the murky waters of the legal profession. After his graduation, he enrolled in Law school, doing his due diligence and advanced as a celebrated Barrister in 1975 as a legal assistant in Sudan before he got promoted into a second-class judge in the judiciary of the Republic of Sudan.

His judiciary journey was nothing like a straight road like they say, a smooth sail does not make the best Sailor, he was also faced with a fair amount of life's ups and downs in his judicial journey. Although, he later became the Mainstream judiciary Judge in former Western Equatoria in 1984 as an acting judge before joining his fellow freedom fighters' countrymen in the bush in the peak of the liberation struggle. Even though he was in the bush fighting for the liberation of his people, Justice Bullen never put out the flame of his legal profession. Asides, being in the bush strategizing about the freedom of his countrymen, he served both as a judge and a soldier. "I handled civil and criminal cases in the SPLA controlled areas. We were running judicial matters in the bush" says the no-nonsense judge. His expertise when it comes to legal matters is not to be questioned as he recalls all the challenging moments in a serial order.

After graduating with Honours in Law from the University of Khartoum, he passed his Barrister Examination to become one of the first batches to be deployed to the judiciary where he served as a legal assistant until 1984 when he resigned as a Presiding Judge in Yambio to join his fellow countrymen in the fight to liberate South Sudan. He joined the Sudan People's Liberation Movement (SPLM). Upon graduating in Bonga in 1985 with Zalzal Division as a Captain and Judicial Officer where he was positioned to several parts of the Upper Nile and Equatoria regions. He later got promoted to an Alternate Commander and then to a full Commander in year 2000. On the official signing of Permanent Ceasefire in 2002 and on Sudan's preparation for running the State, Justice Bullen took a Study Leave and went to Germany to improve his knowledge of Constitutional Law.

"In 1994, when the military was separated after the Chukudum Convention, "I was appointed the Deputy Chief Justice until the commencement of the agreement where I was appointed Justice to the Constitutional Court in Khartoum". Also, in this account, Justice Wol Makach the then Deputy President of the Constitutional Court or Chief Justice of South Sudan, Justice Bullen was appointed Deputy President of the Constitutional court in Khartoum. In the early 2000s after his emancipation from his apprehension and uniting with his family, Justice Bullen with his love for his legal profession proceeded to go to Germany in 2002 after the permanent ceasefire between Northern and Southern Sudan. He obtained an LLM, Constitutional law from his alma mater Heidelberg University, Germany (2002-2003). Then, proceeded to Max Plunk Institute Germany (2003-2004) Fellowship, for Comparative Constitutional and International Law.

In 2011, Justice Bullen was appointed as the Justice of the Supreme Court of South Sudan. According to him "that was an appointment that never went down well with me as I was appointed junior to my juniors. I have more wealth of experience than most of my then superiors". Before the final hit of the gavel i.e. his resignation, Justice Bullen Awal urges the government to intensify more effort into disarming the citizens to accomplish complete peace in South Sudan. *"A larger percentage of the peace process depends on the government and its responsibility to talk to rebel groups, make concessions because it has the resources. More than normal effort is required to achieve peace, the government as a whole must encourage rebels to show up for negotiation and amnesty. A dialogue should*

The Fallen Distinguished Judge: The Constitutional Laws Fundamentalist

hold between the government and rebel, this will not only result in peace but confidence building."

Even though he had what can be considered a rather long reign as the Justice of the Supreme Court, Justice Bullen decided he had had enough of the corruption and prejudices happening in the judicial system. However, not until his resignation, Justice Bullen Awal was the only Judge in the Supreme Court with Retired Major General Rank. A rank which he obtained not from his position agreement but the voluntary Revolutionary Struggle. One would not be wrong to say Justice Bullen Awal had a soft spot for liberators and freedom fighters. He has also had a similar hard experience when he was a little boy in the bush fighting for what's rightfully theirs and their freedom. He takes a keen interest and mostly on the side of liberators especially when they have been sidelined or swindled from their hard-earned freedom or resources.

As a true believer of justice, his passion for the law did not fade out even after his resignation. He joined the South Sudan Bar Association officially- a professional club of legal practitioners. A true follower of due protocols, he formally completed the mandated one-year requirement by the Judiciary Act, 2008. During his interview with Paul Jimbo, he revealed he offers both private and institutional legal consultancy. In his own words, "I can be an advocate in any civil or criminal case because I offer legal advice out of my wealth of experience and deep understanding of the law." Justice Awal says with ease. Honourable Justice Awal practiced law under his firm Alier Gaar Law Firm located in Bor and Juba, however, it does not exclude other parts of Juba. Asides his LLM at the Heidelberg University, Germany, he held a fellowship from Max Plunck Institute of Constitutional Law and International Law (Germany). Whilst in Europe, he earned himself another prestige fellowship to attend University of London where he studied

Advanced Legislative Drafting postgraduate qualification. Before his demise, Justice Awal was expected to be part of Sudan's Honourable reference and guide in legal practice in and outside courts.

The iconic, no-nonsense judge resignation indeed left an indelible stamp in South Sudan's laws, courts, and the understanding of the laws itself. As one of the major contributors to South Sudan's Constitution, he relished his role in the Court. His tough and landmark rulings indeed gained him some opposition and waggling tongues. One of the tough and strict stances he had was being against the civilians being in possession of unlicensed firearms.

Also, he painted a forbidden picture of the country's judiciary and believes that death sentences should be introduced as the penalty for murder cases. His opinion of the introduction of the death sentence penalty could be a major deterrent to the dystrophic state of the nation. According to him, he encourages such an extreme penalty for murder cases as the current situation of the country then does not support consensual cooperation. Hence, if a culprit is found guilty of murder, he needs not to be given any option but the death penalty.

According to REDRESS Arrested Development: Sudan's Constitutional Court, Access to Justice and the Effective Protection of Human Rights (2012), "the death penalty: Sudan is one of the countries with the highest number of capital punishments. Human rights bodies have repeatedly raised concerns over: 'The imposition in the State party of the death penalty for offenses which cannot be characterised as the most serious, including embezzlement by officials, robbery with violence and drug trafficking, as well as practices which should not be criminalised such as committing a third homosexual act and illicit sex, is incompatible with article 6 of the Covenant. (arts. 6 and 7 of the Covenant)'. For Justice Panchol Awal, sentencing culprits for major crimes like murder, terrorism with the intent to kill are grave capital offense which should attract capital punishments.

However, that is not the legacy of Justice Bullen Panchol Awal, he was a firm believer of the law and how to wield it in favour of the constitution in a fair and just cause. As with most messiahs, opposition and unbelief are common stumbling blocks. In the case of Justice Awal, the corruption in the system had eaten deep and he could only muster enough strength and stance so as not to nullify the sacrifices and compromises of those who suffered for South Sudan to gain its full and recognised autonomy and independence.

Justice Bullen Education Summary:

At the formative age, Late Justice Bullen Panchol Awal attended elementary, secondary and tertiary Education in different region of the Sudan and Germany before Independence of South Sudan.

The institutions include: -

- 1957 – 1959: Baidit Bush Primary School.
- 1960 – 1962: Malek Elementary School.
- 1963 - 1965: Obel Junior Secondary School.
- 1966 – 1968: Rumbek Senior Secondary School.
- 1970 – 1975: University of Khartoum, LLB Law Honours.
- 2002 – 2003: Max Plunk Institute (Germany); Fellowship, Comparative Constitutional & International Laws.
- 2003 – 2004: Heidelberg University – Germany (LLM Constitutional Law).
- 2005 – 2006: University of London (Institute of Advanced Legal Studies) – UK (Advanced Legislative Drafting).

CHAPTER THREE
GRADUATION AND WHAT'S NEXT?

Growing up in the days of war, adversity, killings, hunger, and diseases, only one thing was certain – Uncertainty. As a victim of war, you could imagine the wealth of experience and stories Justice Bullen Panchol could have to share. Lots of hurdles did affect his growing up and education, yet he was determined to absorb more education to fight his fight using the right and fair techniques approved in the book of law. He graduated during the First Civil War propagated by the Arabs of Sudan. At that time, hundreds of thousands were displaced and forced to flee their place of solace and community. Others hid in bushes and others who had the means sought refuge in neighbouring countries like Kenya, Ethiopia, Congo, and Uganda.

Many others who were not as privileged or 'lucky' as Young Bullen were victims of the genocides that took place and sadly were victims of crimes, they knew nothing about. Several others who were lucky were separated from their loved ones and had to walk miles, hundreds of miles with their source of strength being only hope. Rather than being consumed in rage, even though everything happening in South Sudan then validates it, he knew he had to get justice for his fellow kinsmen the right way. The Arabs in Old Sudan then, recognised a larger part of South Sudan indigenes were uneducated formally. Hence took advantage of their illiteracy to cheat, displace, and commit other crimes against them. Forcing them to watch as they unlawfully and unjustly exploit their resources, the mining regions in Abyei, Bentiu, Ruweng, Upper Nile and oil exploration without the indigenous owners of the resources benefitting from it.

The Fallen Distinguished Judge: The Constitutional Laws Fundamentalist

The Second Civil War in Old Sudan lasted for 21 years as South Sudan declared war against the government than as a result of the marginalization. During these times, food supplies declined, people could not cultivate their farmlands, hence, the hunger rate increased. Most farmlands were converted to battlefields. Hunger was another form of weapon used by the Arabs on South Sudanese because they were Christians. They declared Jihad in South Sudan and killed lots of innocent lives in remote villages. Malnutrition was common then and a major killer of children, many suffered from kwashiorkor. These and other manmade disasters claimed so many lives in South Sudan. According to statistics, the bloodshed and genocides that happen in South Sudan summed up to more than 2.5 million people. Malaria, Measles, and other diseases were quite rampant, with the overpopulated and underfunded and clinics with little or no hospital resources to take better care of patients. Those living closer to the Nile River were more vulnerable to mosquito bites during the rainy season.

During the war, seeing dead bodies and human remains seem to be the order of the day and nothing new to refugees. Most teenagers and youths had nothing to cling to but hope and in constant fear of their lives, the elderly was not spared either. Some were lucky to listen to war tales, some witnessed the killings of their loved ones, while others saw as life left the body of their families either through genocide, hunger, or other manmade or war-influenced factors. Till these days, some suffered the PTSD of witnessing live executions, or how certain parts of their bodies were damaged as a result of explosions.

For young Bullen Panchol, he had the opportunity others could only dream of having but used it to save others. After completing his Bar exams, he got employed as a legal assistant. Learning on the job theoretically and practically. He understood how pragmatic he needed to be to get justice for the sufferings of his people. While still maintaining his position in the courtroom, he enrolled in the military. For many, handling two demanding professions and contrast forms of government pertaining to law and order, young Bullen Panchol was quite focused and impressive. Within a few years of enrolling in the military, he became a Captain after graduating in Bonga with the Zalzal Division in 1984. His achievement was not only limited to the military grounds, in his chosen profession, but he also earned his place to the Presiding Judge before retiring in 1984 in Yambio Constitutional Court. He achieved these in the space of 9 years i.e. 1975-1984. Asides from being patriotic and transparent, one would not be wrong to refer to Judge Bullen Awal as a dogmatic achiever and a go-getter. Not being complacent with his current achievements then, he proceeded with his resignation to join the SPLA.

SUDAN PEOPLE'S LIBERATION ARMY (SPLA)

SPLA now known as South Sudan People's Defense Forces (SSPDF) is the recognised army of South Sudan. Founded as a revolutionary movement against the oppressive government of Sudan in 1983 and a major participant of the Sudanese Second Civil War which was championed by Dr. John Garang. The SPLA came into existence as a result of a couple of rebellion in May 1983 (now considered SPLA Day, a public holiday in South Sudan) that broke out in the military barracks of the Sudanese army in the southern regions especially Bor, Pibor, Ayod, etc. The rebellions were planned and executed by Major Alier Nhial Mangardit and Major Kerubino Kuanyin Bol, the aftermath of the rebellion led to the establishment of SPLA. In June 1983, most of the rebellions had moved to Ethiopia still in transit. The Ethiopian government decided to give support to the new force as a means of exacting vendetta on the Sudanese government for its supports of Eritrean rebels against the Ethiopian government.

The SPLA struggled for a secular and most importantly united Sudanese state. Dr. John Garang believed the struggle of the South Sudanese state is not more different than that of the relegated groups (Fur and Nuba) in the north. Not until 1985 did SPLA directed its public denouncements of the Sudanese government at Nimeri. In the following years, SPLA propaganda publicly condemned the Khartoum government as a family affair that influenced sectarian tensions. At the end of September 1983, the denouncement of SPLA led to the introduction of Sharia Law.

The 1980s were pretty much a challenging time for the people of South Sudan. The SPLA complete battalion graduated in 1984 in the village of Bilpam. To this day, the name Bilpam carries important symbolic importance for SPLA as it identifies as the epicentre of their coming to being. Other SPLA training camps were created at Bonga, Dimma, and Panyido. In 1985, Judge Bullen resigned from his legal and military positions to be recruited as a soldier for the SPLA. Although, we cannot say for certain if Judge Bullen took part in the siege and blockage of developmental projects of Sudanese government such as the Bentiu Oil Fields and Jonglei. In 1985-1986, SPLA launched its campaign advance in Equatoria, as expected they were confronted by a handful of pro-government rebels.

SPLA and Anyanya II

Both parties had a complicated relationship between 1984 and 1987. The Anyanya II forces hindered the SPLA expansion, as they frequently attacked the SPLA recruits on their way to Ethiopia. Anyanya II attacked civilians who they believed to be supporters of SPLA. Considered to have some political affiliation, the conflict between Anyanya II & SPLA that is, the Anyanya II was seeking to build an independent South Sudanese state. To put an end to the bloodshed and conflict, the SPLA tried to sway in the leaders of Anyanya

II, in late 1987, the commander of Anyanya II Commander Gordon Kong Chuol aligned with their terms and conditions. As expected, other sectors of Anyanya II allied with the Sudanese government followed the example of the commander. The rebellion laid the small town of Kurmuk near the Ethiopian border in November of 1987. The village was 450 miles away from the country's capital, its nearby the dam which supplied Khartoum with a large portion of its electricity. It was at this point the Sudanese government felt more pressure and nervous towards containing the SPLA. Before that the SPLA had victorious conquers, as the rebellion kept on growing with more improvement in their growing and discipline.

According to his interview with Mading Ngor Akec earlier in 2020, Judge Bullen Panchol was in the bush fighting for the freedom and rights of his people for 21 years. He witnessed the boycotting of 1986 by the SPLA, this resulted in the election not holding in more than half of southern Sudan constituencies. The Revolutionary Command Council (RCC) invited SPLA to a 'National dialogue conference' in September 1989, the SPLA decided not to attend. However, in 1988, the SPLA and the Democratic Unionist Party entered into a long-standing peace deal on November 15, 1988 by entering into an alliance to abolish sharia law and declare a state of emergency. It was announced to the public on Radio SPLA. After DUP rejoined the Sudanese government, a ceasefire was accomplished. However, negotiations between Sadiq al-Mahdi and SPLA was brought to a rather abrupt end after SPLA gun down a civilian airplane, causing the death of more than 50 people.

Although still optimistic about the peace agreement holding water, the Nation Islamic Front (NIF) coup d'état in 1989 prompted any peace talks to be on hold. The SPLA launched a new attack capturing towns like Bor, Kaya, Yambio, Torit, Akobo, Nasir, Maridi, etc. Before mid-year of 1991, SPLA had gained full control over most southern Sudanese states except major garrison towns like Yei, Juba, and Wau. In the early months of 1990 particularly January 21 and 29, SPLA opened fire on Juba and moved into other southern regions like Blue Nile State and Nuba mountains. As compared to the early days of the exploit of SPLA, they are now better organised in their conduct.

For most youths, what comes next after schooling, securing quite a comfortable job that syncs with one's passion, settling down seems to be the next thing. Although Judge Bullen Panchol married and gave birth to his first son in the late 1979, he still recognised although his first duty is to his family. In as much as his family is comfortable to live in a country without being in constant fear of being abducted or worse killed, he owed a great duty to his country and his kinsmen, hence why he spent 21 years in the bush fighting for the freedom of his people.

Trouble began to brew for the SPLA in the 1990s as the Ethiopian government that provides the SPLA with a significant amount of support experienced downfall which resulted in a major setback. For 18 years the Ethiopian government was the supplier of training facilities, safe haven, and military supplies for the SPLA. After powered changes hands in the Ethiopia government, the SPLA led hundreds of thousands of refugees back into Sudan. During these times, the leadership of Dr. Garang was brought to questioning as a split had been seethed in the late 1990s. Dr. Lam Akol began making plans to sway in SPLA officers to embrace his quest especially the Shilluk and Nuer people.

The Nasir Declaration came about in 1991, the split situation had already taken enough form and the Ethiopian/Derg regime had completely been shattered. Dr. Akol made good use of the opportunity to publish an article instigating the impeachment of Dr. Garang, the article was titled "Why

Garang must go". The nonconformists moved the motion of democratising SPLA to champion an independent South Sudan and to put a final stop to human rights abuses. During this time, the SPLA experienced chaos in their camp as there was no distinct clarification of what unit supports Dr. Garang or Dr. Akol SPLA-Nasir. The split did not only cause war, it led to the two factions attacking civilians who they believe belonged to their opponent's turf.

The split weakened the SPLA, hence making it easy for the Sudanese government to launch an attack against the SPLA, this resulted in the SPLA losing control of Bor, their headquarter Torit, Pochalla, and Kapoeta in 1992. During this time, Judge Bullen took his family to the border of Uganda for a safer abode. He and his two wives late Ayak Agok Guor, Aluel Biar Deng-aguek and their little children.

CHAPTER FOUR
SOUTH SUDAN'S INDEPENDENCE & THE AFTERMATH: THE JUDICIAL CHALLENGES AND CHANGES.

South Sudan is one of the youngest nations in the world. After gaining its independence on the 9th of July 2011, many South Sudanese citizens were hopeful for a new beginning, ready to forget the pain and ineptitude of past leaderships. However, what seems to be much-anticipated emancipation was just a tragic return of violence and conflict, even though everyone hoped South Sudan was on the road to development and institutions building. After decades of instability, and almost being robbed off of their territory. South Sudan became an independent sovereign state, but it was born prematurely into a conflict state where their instability became obvious through various challenges. Even though South Sudan voted for sovereignty via referendum with President Omar Bashir acknowledging the result, the hopeful road to independence was plagued by unresolved issues relating to border defining, distribution of oil revenues, and establishing laws particularly South Sudanese constitution which Justice Bullen Panchol played a critical role in this aspect.

Although South Sudan fulfilled all its declarative requirements according to international law, the resources required to build an independent state were lacking, hence leading South Sudan into another phase of civil war and dystopia. Most of the conflicts stem from political violence, corrupted leadership in Juba, war mongers, belly development behaviours, corrupted judiciary system, nepotism, poor infrastructure, and possession of firearms by the average citizen illegally, making it difficult for South Sudan to gain control over its territory and moving forward as a nation. The legacies of the prolonged civil war including unresolved issues within the Comprehensive Peace Agreement, politico-military incongruent policies, and communal violence present serious challenges to the Government of South Sudan as it struggles to sustain its independence (Wassara, S. (2015).

More to the point, South Sudan continued to experience severe conflicts particularly as a result of ethnic division, poor governance, etc. Few days after gaining its independence as a sovereign state, the young country experienced vile deadly attacks in two regions with the highest ethnic mix particularly around the north-south border hence putting the Sudanese peace process to test. Before the vote of the referendum was fully considered, on July 7, 2011, a transitional Constitution was approved by political leaders and legislative heads where Justice Bullen Panchol was actively involved in the composition. As a country born out of limited human capital and into weak institutions, hence making it unfit for sustainable economic growth and development. South Sudan is largely fragmented ethnically, where each ethnic group is after maximising their own objectives which may in the long run weaken the government to work on the amalgamation of all ethnicities.

For South Sudan, its first independence anniversary was tensed with complex challenges especially the fight over the common border of the Republic of Sudan. During this time, the conflicts were the top priority of the government hence diverting their attention to concentrating on major issues like human development and economic growth. For years, the non-consensual marriage between South Sudan and the Republic of Sudan, the culmination stemmed out of the demand to be autonomous to which the people of South Sudan had high hopes for the dissolution of both countries will bring a complete end to the conflicts. A year post-independence not much has happened in South Sudan except for the unexpected downward trends stemmed from complete distrust from both countries prolonged conflict with hope for a better future almost fading away. The absence of good relations lowered the probability of negotiating a thorough dialogue, and much more settlement.

FIRST YEAR POST-INDEPENDENCE

One major cause of mistrust and unrest post-independence was rooted in the sources of irreconcilable differences that resulted in the culmination of North and South Sudan that were not completely resolved before the separation. In essence, prior to South Sudan's independence, both countries had not reached a consensus on how to control issues that makes them an entity even after Sudan's independence. External factors also played an active role in the conflict between the two countries particularly factors whose interest does not align with either of the two countries but further complicates the situation hence making it difficult for both South Sudan and the Republic of Sudan.

South Sudan has numerous natural resources, particularly a significant amount of the country's oil deposits is scattered along the border of both countries. Therefore, making the need to draft a contending and strong policy towards effective management of natural resources was imperative as at then. Determining the ownership of the oil deposits would help both countries proceed with their country's development plans. So, not until the boundary is well-defined, policy initiatives in South Sudan will continue to suffer underdevelopment as a result of conflict over border and resources management. Although the interim natural resource management policy that was utilised prior to South Sudan independence (2007-2011) was initiated by the Government of South Sudan (GoSS). The initiative was created and focused more on land, water, and oil extraction; however, the policy caused more difficulty for South Sudan particularly in the area of property rights in a new nation. Even to date, the management of South Sudan will definitely benefit greatly from more polishing or finesse to stay clear of future conflict. The Republic of Sudan and South Sudan concentrated on more policy effort on the mining and development of the surplus non-renewable resource (oil) but neglecting other resources that are critical to the economic and political development of the nation which is critical for the sustainable and balanced economy of both countries.

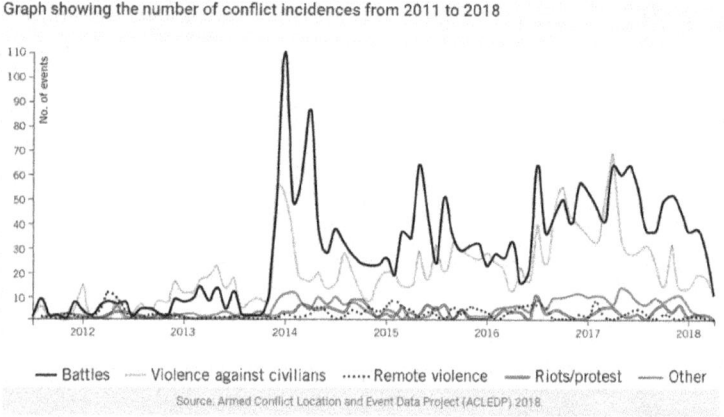

Graph showing the number of conflict incidences from 2011 to 2018

Source: Armed Conflict Location and Event Data Project (ACLEDP) 2018.

Attacks were mostly targeted on armless civilians, an increase in gender-based violence especially rape, kidnapping, murder, and razing down homes was the order of the day post-independence. Convoys bringing in aid materials were looted and attacked by rebels, about 50% of all pupils who were eligible to be within the four walls of a classroom were pulled out of school according to UNICEF. The dystopia was not confined in formal settings but also extended into the rural areas and most farmers and unskilled workers who had fled their place of business only to scavenge for other means of survival. The current state of South Sudan is considered to be one of the worst in the world. This was as a result of the accumulated disadvantage of over four decades of war.

Still on record that before the celebrations of its newly gained independence, South Sudan was experiencing a brewing civil war due to the lack of sufficient time to create response mechanisms, laws, policies, institutions, etc. that may lower the potential effects of war. South Sudan was considered one of the most fragile countries according to the World Index, which may collapse due to constant pressure and dystopia of war. According to Reuters 2017b, the budget needed to cater to the crisis in 2017 to 7.6 million internally displaced citizens was about $1.7 billion, but only 73% of the budget was financed. The same fate occurred in 2018, prompting aid agencies to call for help amongst willing private sectors for adequate funding. Yet, the shortage of funds was principal as a result of the flamboyant lifestyle of the corrupt politicians and lawmakers (Waal, 2014).

International communities and aid agencies chose not to relent in the mobilising of humanitarian and diplomatic resources to respond to immediate needs, protect natives of South Sudan, and ultimately seek for ways to put an end to the conflicts. Regions under the sponsorships of Intergovernmental Authority Development (IGAD), pioneered the effort to arbitrate between North and South Sudan with the backing of Africa Union (AU), International partners, Security Council, and the United Nations (UN). The African Union has contributed immensely even though its involvement via the AU Commission of Inquiry was an essential role in examining the root causes of conflict and proffering solutions for institutional reforms and accountability as a nation.

The United Nation's Security Council tried to find ways to improve the region's effort so as to enable a feasible political solution to the conflict including via the threat of sanctions and has approved the deployment of additional peacekeepers in the bid to protect civilians and to support the peace process, and humanitarian relief processes. In 2015, South Sudan replaced Afghanistan as the most corrupt country with the most fragile state of peace. With over 60 deaths of relief workers recorded since the commencement of conflict, one could deduce the killings were staged premeditated to hinder the supply of relief materials to certain communities. The Secretary-General of the United Nations at the time mentioned his grave concerns especially the issue of restriction access and roadblocks "harassment and attempt by officials and restricted movement". He also stated that "despite government claims to the contrary, I believe this environment of impunity and intimidation is deliberate and not just a consequence of growing criminality." The Panel of Experts of the United Nations reported the threats against the international humanitarian body and U.N. personnel are rapidly hitting a high number and grave degree of brutality where senior officials are increasing their oratory speeches against brutality and hostility towards the aid agencies, and the broader international community.

PEACE DEVELOPMENTS IN SOUTH SUDAN TILL DATE.

Since the collapse of the 2016 peace agreement, the civil war in South Sudan has been quite tenacious. All efforts during this time have been made to pull leaders to the negotiating table, however, all proved abortive. In the early days of May 2018, peace talks resumed in Addis Ababa, however by the end of May, the meetings got concluded with no form of a formal agreement. Both SPLM-IO rebel faction led by Dr.Riek Machar and South Sudan government rejected the proposals by IGAD on the basis of sharing government positions, security arrangements, and the governing system of the country. However, in June 2018, the pressure got to its peak hence increasing the need for President Salva Kiir and Dr. Riek Machar to meet for the first time in two years, the meeting was held in Khartoum. Fortunately, the meeting ended with the signing of a new peace agreement that called for the nation's cease-fire and the distribution of government positions.

However, an hour after the cease-fire was announced, it was violated in the northern part of the country, but both the rebels and government accused one another of violating the peace agreement. This leaves room for analysts to be sceptical of whether the newly signed agreements will be honoured.

One of the major factors that threaten this new agreement is the creation of four vice-president positions at once, as well as efforts to lengthen the presidential term again by another three years (this is as a result of the absence of election in 2015 which was not conducted). Other areas of concern that threatened the agreement were the resumption of oil explorations in which opposing parties expressed their dissatisfaction. Asides the cease-fire, the agreement stated a 120-day pre-transition period as well as a 36-month transition which was to be followed by a general election, and the withdrawal of troops from villages, camps, urban areas, churches, and schools. Worth mentioning is the fact that external groups have found ways to negotiate and also share the parliamentary and executive positions shared by the two main characters. The agreement was signed on 8th July 2018 in Kampala Uganda in their presence, therefore earning them a position in the four positions proposed in for the vice-presidency of South Sudan. Although the peace agreement signed was a welcomed move, it does not satisfactorily deal with the root causes of the fallouts of previous peace agreements.

STATE OF THE JUDICIARY POST INDEPENDENCE

The judiciary state of South Sudan post-independence was like other systems and infrastructure, it was poorly developed and in a rut. For the longest time since independence, South Sudan's judiciary system was in a corruption-ridden and messy state. Rather than building a new South Sudan with the exposure and hope of a new beginning, many policymakers turned out to be interested in selfish, belly-infrastructure, making a ruling that favours not just their pockets but for venal reasons. According to Justice Bullen Panchol, the judiciary system of South Sudan needed to have a unanimous voice against corruption and nepotism. Although, there are lapses as regards the official language which is to be used in the courtroom. For instance, the constitution had some written in Arabic interpretation clauses, some laws are not befitting for the current trends of the world, hence making some of the laws in the constitution obsolete. The judiciary system of South Sudan also suffered heavily from incompetency as it was evident inexperienced lawyers were given the highest positions in the judiciary e.g. there were cases were incompetent and incapacitated lawyers were installed as Chief Justice to hinder any progressive change that can bring about rapid political and socio-economic development to South Sudan.

Justice Bullen Panchol argued that South Sudan's judiciary is wealthy enough to fund its development independently via reserves, levies, stamp duty charges, and other revenue channels. However, these funds were being looted by top right-wing leaders that held a position closer to the Chief Justice and presidency. He also highlighted the confusion when it comes to sanctions as there are no clear distinctions on whose leadership pronouncement holds the highest power as both the President and Chief Justice contradicts their judgment on almost everything in spite of the existence of an operational constitution. As described by Justice Bullen, the judiciary was more of a figurehead than an actual arm of government as the other arms of government were not ready to accept changes. Nepotism and corruption were the order of the day and had gone beyond redeemable control, these were part of the inherent reasons Justice Bullen Panchol resigned from the judiciary governance system. He had an admirably huge vision for the judiciary of South Sudan, he was motivated for an excellent mission for a properly structured judiciary system, and however, it was hindered by corrupt

The Fallen Distinguished Judge: The Constitutional Laws Fundamentalist

elites. He garnered resources that had great potentials and insights on how well-informed judges can enact great laws and policies that will reflect his passion for change as well as his vision for an improved judiciary system.

Another Judge of similar trait of fairness and an oratory combative style argument permissible in the courtroom was Justice Antonin Scalia – A Supreme Court Justice in America. He was known for his firm and strong opinions and easily influences the courtroom without a single question. Although he was the son of an Italian immigrant born in Trenton, New Jersey, he developed to take the American judicial system by storm with not only his colourful personality but his conservative views. One of his similar traits with Justice Bullen was Judicial Activism and Originalism. Originalism in the sense that judges should extract constitutional decisions based on the 18th century understanding of the constitution. However, one will argue if those 'texts' cannot still be applicable in the present. The originalism is more of an orthodoxy concept. Similarly, Justice Bullen was an activist for a well-structured judiciary system for South Sudan, he was all for connecting law and order to the society at large and promoting a perfect cohesion within the judiciary system. He concerned his reign as the supreme chief justice of South Sudan on better governance, formulating beneficial policies to the people of South Sudan as well as championing the vision of a better independent judiciary system.

As man vast in the knowledge of lawmaking and was once active in the freedom fighting movement of South Sudan, Justice Bullen was appointed by Dr. Garang to be part of comprehensive peace agreement negotiations between Government of Sudan – Khartoum led government and then Southern Sudan rebel to bring about a wave of lasting peace in Kenya. The former Sudanese rebel and former first Vice President Dr. Garang de Mabior would consult with the late Judge first before progressing with any rebel movement agenda. Even though on some proposals they were both in consensus while on some, they fiercely disagree, notwithstanding Dr. Garang appreciated his critical thinking and smartness, and ultimately his transparency and straightforwardness. Justice Bullen was widely recognised as South Sudan's Laws father or South Sudan's Laws Fundamentalist. He was branded the "no-nonsense Judge" which was a result of his stern decisions. The late Judge was appointed as the head of South Sudan's constitutional review in 2005, prior to the signing of the peace agreement.

Noting that South Sudan gained its sovereignty in the 21st century with enough exposure to the current trends in nation-building, best policies, it was expected that enormous effort should be put into the development of the world's newest nation. The top leadership seemed to fail in handling the root causes of conflict such as border demarcation, resource ownership, and management, yet corrupt politicians were more concerned about their selfish agendas, hence blocking positive change. Justice Bullen as well as most South Sudan's at large hoped for nepotism and corrupt-free new South Sudan. It became imperative for the judiciary to step up to their parliamentary rights and influence by charging corrupt lawmakers, however, this held no water as the judiciary had fewer independent rights as compared to the presidency, hence contradiction of laws and policies was the order of the day. However, Justice Bullen Panchol gave the corrupt practices and judges a hard time, hence earning him the name "no-nonsense" judge. He was not afraid nor timid to exhibit the rare traits of humility, integrity, professionalism, and nobility.

THE INTERIM CONSTITUTION

South Sudan's Interim Constitution was introduced in 2005. Part 7 of the Interim constitution created the independent Judiciary. Justice Bullen played a major role in the composition of the judiciary arm of Sudan's government. It established that the judiciary is in charge of the maintenance and professional training standard for elected or appointed judicial personnel. The judiciary was made up of the Supreme Court, High Courts, Court of Appeal, and County Courts. Noteworthy, the fact that the constitution calls for the significant representation of women in the judiciary. The Interim Constitution was adopted following the regaining of autonomous status and the Comprehensive Peace Agreement (CPA). Its purpose was to govern the transition period between the referendum and the CPA period. The interim constitution created distinct boundaries between Northern and Southern Sudan, even though the constitution was laid open to the laws of Sudan as at then. The Interim Constitution created a presidential system of government with the three arms of government. The head of government – President is the Head of State, Head of Government, and Commander-in-Chief. The constitution also explicitly established South Sudan as a decentralised nation with ten states.

TRANSITIONAL CONSTITUTION

On July 9th, 2011 – South Sudan's independence, South Sudan replaced its interim constitution with the Transitional Constitution of South Sudan. Drafted and reviewed by a selected few technical review committees with zero interference or participation of the public. The process commenced on the 21st of January 2011 with the consent and decree of the presidency. Primarily, the Transitional Constitution was majorly on the revision of the Interim Constitution for the aim of screening out redundancies and references to a united Sudan as a sovereign state. Upon final submission of the draft, it was sent to the then 'Office of the Presidency of Southern Sudan' with the proposals of the technical committee for creating a permanent political deed. After the endorsement of the Transitional Constitution, the international critics and opposition parties cautioned that way too much power was bestowed in the hands of the President and Central government. In total contrast, the then Minister of Information stated that "people of South Sudan were consulted via the representative in the parliament". The Chairperson of Information, Culture, and Communications Committee of the Parliament averred that the Transitional Constitution "represents the rights and will of the people of South Sudan".

According to the Transitional Constitution, the executive power resides with the President who is also the Commander-in-Chief of SPLA and the Supreme Commander or other armed forces. Amid lots of influence, power, and responsibilities, the President appointed several officials, hence extending his influence all through the important institutions of the country. For instance, in the Judiciary, the President appoints the Chief Justice and Deputy, as well as judges in the statutory courts. In the same vein, the President also possesses the full power to remove the individual from appointed positions as a result of some serious misconduct. South Sudan operates under a bicameral legislature i.e. 50-seat Council of states, 332-seat National Legislative Assembly where each member serves the country in their assigned capacity for a four-year term. South Sudan comprises of 10 states and now 3 Administrative Areas to which each state is governed by a governor-elect, state cabinets, and state legislative assemblies. Each of these states has its constitution and pass laws so long they conform to the Transitional Constitution. To a certain degree, the new Constitution the Head of State can denunciate or remove a state governor and/or disband a state legislative assembly in the event of a dystopic environment that threatens territorial integrity and national security. In this case, a caretaker governor is then charged with preparing for elections. None of these provisions were in writing in the Interim Constitution.

Transiting from the Interim Constitution to the Transitional Constitution looked simple on paper but there were obvious inherent constitutional challenges, hence constitutional review was adopted. However, compounding the issues and delays that accompany the process of reviewing the constitution, another bone of contention was the increasing rate of corruption in the public sector. It was discovered that the sum of $2.5 billion was embezzled from the state, hence invoking anger on several South Sudanese. Another important review of the constitution was demanding the law enacting the safety of the girl-child by stating an official marriageable age to promote the education of the girl child. Women groups championed this movement to prompt the inclusion in the reviewed Transitional Constitution.

The Transitional Constitution is to remain in force until the adoption of a permanent constitution. To this end, it provided for a National Constitutional Review Commission to be established within six months of independence. The President was entitled to appoint its members, after due consultation with the political parties, civil society, and other stakeholders. The main tasks of the Commission were, first, to review the Transitional Constitution, after having collected views and suggestions from "all stakeholders", with a view to "including any changes that may need to be introduced to the current system of governance" and second, to raise awareness on constitutional issues, involving the general public. Subsequently, the then Vice-President called upon South Sudanese civil society to submit the names of four additional potential members of the Commission. This opening to civil society did not prevent further accusations of lack of transparency, with the Government also accused of repeating the same errors committed with the adoption of the Interim Constitution and Transitional Constitution by favouring over-representation of the SPLM (International Commission of

Jurists, 2013).

On a final note, the state of the judiciary as described by Late Justice Bullen Panchol during his interview with Mading Ngor Akec on Fixing Sudan episode. He stated one of the problems of the modern judiciary of South Sudan is the type of personnel appointed into the judiciary. He further clarified that, there were people who create ideas that have great potential in creating beneficial institutions while there some that are redundant. Also, certain elected judges lack the correct vision for the judiciary. The official language in South Sudan is English, however, there are still sitting judges of over 10 years who still attend to court cases in Arabic, hence conveying the failure in the judiciary in compliance with current world trends and as it applies to the operating laws in South Sudan. The failure to transform the institutions by training them the laws in English will not increase better administering of justice to the people of South Sudan. He further recommended the restructuring of the judiciary by attracting qualified human resource i.e. lawyers and judges, putting them under qualitative control, and particularly controlling the revenue-generating aspect of the judiciary.

The absence of proper leadership in the judiciary makes it difficult to control the justice system, revenue-generating, arm, and enacting proper sanctions and laws. He also emphasised the independence of the judiciary, i.e. leaving judges to pass judgments without interference from the Presidency to the best of their conscience and as recognised and permitted by the constitution. Upon resignation, Justice Panchol asserted he still had faith in South Sudan's judiciary but highly concerned about what is happening in all arms of government as it seems those who fought for the sovereignty of the country died in vain as South Sudan was still in a state of burgeoning chaos.

The Independent Cornerstone of Government of South Sudan Mounted with Law Problems: Judge Bullen's Alier Gaar Law Firm

Government in any society is a complicated thing for any ordinary citizen. In South Sudan, with our system of checks of balances between three powerful wings of central government layered on top of ten individual state governments and three administrative areas , each of which handles their checks and balances in an individual ways, our government which is summarised as of the people, by the people and for the people has become a phenomenally complex and complicated thing in Juba.

After over ten years of history, it's amazing to see that this government that rules the current South Sudan is still very much the product of those cornerstone documents that were written by the founding fathers like Justice Bullen Panchol Awal, the Constitution, the Bill of Rights and especially the Declaration of Independence. The national sense of self and that distinctively South Sudanese personality is very much interwoven with the bold statements in these documents.

For one thing, South Sudanese have an intrinsic sense of their own rights and their ability to function separate from government. As such, government is never outside of the critical scrutiny of the people that it rules. While this seems perfectly normal to the citizens of this country, it is uncommon historically where government ruled with virtual absolute authority and the people were subservient to their leaders. To a South Sudanese, the ones they elect to serve work for the public. And if they ever forget that or appear to be attempting to gather more power than they are allowed, it isn't long before the leadership of the country is replaced. This ability of the people to peaceably throw the bums out and bellies forward has kept government in check and constantly on edge for. And that is a good thing.

The Declaration of Independence would have to be considered a cornerstone of how our system of government works because along with independence from Sudan, that document created a spirit of independence and pride in the South Sudan psyche that has influenced virtually every aspect of both public and private life. When South Sudan declared itself independent from Sudan in 2011, it firmly entrenched into the soul of every South Sudanese to never be dependent on any other country, government or ruler ever again.

To an outsider, the fierce dedication to freedom and self-determination that is so deeply entrenched in South Sudanese culture seems peculiar. But that fundamental conviction that we are a free people, not just of tyranny from without but free of oppression from within as well affects every aspect of South Sudanese life. That sense of self will, and self-awareness is what makes South Sudanese music, movies, cultural life and art to exciting and addictive around East Africa and the world.

There was something buried in that bold declaration to the cruelty that we would be an independent and free people that changed the personality of South Sudan forever. We did not just break away to be adrift from our point of origin, in this case The Khartoum. Rather when we declared freedom, it was not just freedom from oppression and the dominance of government, it was freedom to greatness that rose up out of the people, not from a government that was the keeper of the people.

The Declaration of Independence accomplished its short-term goal of changing the culture of what was happening on the Sudanese mainland from a bold act of colonisation into an even bolder building of a new nation. But accomplished so much more by putting a determination in the heart and soul of every South Sudanese to never again be subjects of a government. Instead government in this new country would forever be the subject of the people, their servant and answerable to them. So South Sudanese keep their government on a long leash, the other way around. This is a revolutionary concept and one that has not been working well for over ten years becoming the envy of greedy leaders all around the country.

Can South Sudan Citizens Check Term Limits Pro and Con for a Nation?

When South Sudan got independent as young nation, if we could have put any sign on the shores of the country for any foreign government to read, it might have said No Kings kind of ruling Allowed! The conviction was strong that this new country would never be a place where royalty dominated the people and were held up for worship as was the abuse in so many countries we see in Africa and Middle East.

So many of the protections that were put in place in our founding documents were put there to assure that it would be virtually impossible for anyone to become king in South Sudan. No matter how much power a politician or legislative body were able to amass, our system of government made sure that no one party, person or special interest group would be able to hold power forever and that no one could take over the government, stage a coup and change South Sudan into a tyrannical monarchy like we had left behind in Sudan.

Justice Bullen Panchol Awal always stressed that, the separation of powers between the executive, the legislative and the judicial is one of the protections we need in place to make sure no single part of the government can arrest total power from the other two. And while this separation has led to plenty of friction and battles between the branches of government, that is exactly the way it should be. Better to fight it out and have a government of shared power than to have one branch that make all the decisions and rule like a king like this government of President Kiir Mayardit.

Just as important to the preservation of our unique governmental system is the use of term limits to restrict the extent to which a politician can take up residence in a political office. We are most aware of term limits at the presidential level where we do not allow any one president to serve more than two terms, but the South Sudanese citizens have not realised this dream come true. To some, that should be cut back to one term per president. But the term limit system will probably remain as it is for a long time to come if permanent constitution is enacted.

This issue can generate a considerable amount of emotional debate. And of course, in a free society, political debate is healthy too. How you feel about presidential term limits may have more to do with how much you do or don't like the current president. If you like him a great deal, you would probably cheer for the abolition of term limits entirely. And if you oppose the current occupant of J-ONE, just one term is probably too much. There are some compelling reasons on both side of the argument.

We do trade away a certain amount of experience when we require by law that our current leadership retire after eight years. Next time a new president settles into J-ONE there is a time of learning while that new leadership gets organised and learns how to do this unusual job. Some would argue that forcing leadership from office may be undemocratic because it denies the people the right to return a president to office if he is doing a good job and should continue in leadership.

One visible downside of term limits is that when a politician is in their last term, there is a time of lame duck leadership because that leader no longer has to work hard to win another election. That leader could become reckless and not provide the quality of service to the country that we expect from our leadership.

But our founding fathers wisely believed in the concept of citizen leadership. Their original vision for the presidency would be that a citizen would go to Juba and serve in the office for a season and then quietly return to private practice to let another citizen lead for a while. While our approach to our first president doesn't exactly fit that mould, our system is unfaithful to that vision.

Term limits keeps a constant flow of fresh leadership coming in. Some would say we should tighten term limits at the parliamentarians and maybe even the judicial level. And there are merits to arguments on both sides of that issue. But we can say with assurance that term limits and the other provisions the founding founders put in place has not kept our approach to government true to their vision of how this country would be run. And that means President Kiir as a King is Allowed!

Can South Sudanese Keep Trade Secret?

Transparency is a term that gets used on media platforms a lot as something desirable, particularly in government terms to require that that our elected officials are being open and honest. What transparency means is that there is nothing hidden and the people employing the elected official have complete knowledge of what is going on at all times.

Sometimes we think that even in the world of business, transparency would be a good policy as well. Very often the consumer world gets suspicious that businesses are not doing business in an honest and forthright fashion. But it is not uncommon for a business to have a need to sustain a certain level of secrecy about their products, their marketing and their business plans. This is not always because the business is crooked. It is just a fact of life in the business world and one that has given us a legal framework for trade secrets and confidentiality agreements of various sorts.

What would be the circumstances that you would want to take advantage of the legal status of trade secrets to keep the internal operations of your government business a secret? Well, the most common rational for utilising legal trade secret protection is to retain the marketing advantage that you might have to stay one step ahead of your competition in the region. The world of business can be a cut-throat environment to be sure. If one country competitor in East Africa learns of the secrets of how the competition makes a better product in South Sudan, utilises a superior distribution or marketing plan or has an organisational philosophy that gives them the edge, the competition is more than happy to exploit that knowledge to capture business away. So, it's in the best interest of any government business to protect their advantages from becoming well known to make sure they can capitalise on their hard-earned edge in East Africa competitive market as they deserve to do.

Countries trade secrets generally fall into either the technical or business-related categories. Countries technical trade secrets, as the name implies, are discoveries or new ways of doing things to create something new in your own country. This would include the technical plans or specifications for a protected product or new design, the methods you have designed for manufacturing a breakthrough technology, notes and insider design documentation on failures in testing that would tip off competition on how you innovated this new product.

Government business trade secrets are just as valuable because they include exclusive management and organisational methods that make you more profitable, marketing plans that would give your country competition a heads up on where you are going to hit them, information about your customers and details about your employees and specialised talent that you retain to make your country business technocrats run better than the competition.

There is a lot of corporate espionage between countries to crack the secrecy of other countries to gain a competitive advantage. But as a new country just putting together plans for security, there are a few things you can do to legally protect yourself. A common practice for country businesses in need of trade secret protection is to have their business partners all sign what is called a Nondisclosure agreement which basically requires that anything your partners learn about your country business will remain a trade secret even if the partner relationship does not continue. This is a legally binding document you can use if that partner uses or leaks your trade secrets and you lose business or market advantage from it.

Many countries businesses require similar kinds of documents from employees and even add a non-compete agreement to make sure an employee or partner doesn't use trade secret information to compete for business from them. Your country top law firm can help you decide what is the best way to protect country businesses business and how to use these documents wisely.

South Sudan's Controversial Punishment of the Death Penalty: Judge Bullen Panchol Argument

In the day in day out creation and enforcement of laws by South Sudan government and law enforcement officials, it is a common occurrence for an issue to come up that is layered with emotional and moral questions. At the legislative level even today, South Sudan government is wrestling with issues involving cattle rustlers and rebellions and trying to find a middle ground between the ethical, moral and religious issues versus the peace benefit that might come from the practice.

One of the great debates has been ongoing in South Sudanese society over its history has been over whether it's moral and right to use the death penalty as a punishment for heinous crimes like child abduction and cattle rustling? Whether one is for abolishing this form of punishment or on the side of using it as a just outcome for a criminal, there is no question that the issue itself is a difficult one to decide.

The arguments for or against the death penalty are often not offered from a legal point of view. The positions taken by those both for and against the law fall under a few general classifications:

- The argument from morality against the death penalty. That it's immoral for a just society to take a life, even if it is of a criminal who themselves have taken life.
- The argument from morality for the death penalty. That it's just for the life of one convicted of a heinous crime to lose their lives as a proper outcome of that crime. That certain crimes should always be defined as so grievous that the one committing this crime must not continue to live and that it is the responsibility of the legal system to

remove such individuals from society via the death penalty.
- The argument that the death penalty does or does not constitute cruel or unusual punishment.
- The argument that God calls for the death of the murderer under the and eye for an eye statute from the Hebrew Old Testament.
- The argument that God calls for the forgiveness of even the murderer as part of the theology of the Christian New Testament.
- The argument from economy that it costs less to execute a criminal than to keep him or her in prison for life.
- The argument that the most heinous criminal could be rehabilitated to become a productive member of society.
- The argument from revenge, that the family of victims of heinous crimes deserve to see the killers of their loved ones executed especially Murle cattle rustlers and child abductors.
- The argument from closure that for those same families and for society, seeing the death of a heinous criminal aids in the grief process by providing closure when we see the guilty properly punished.

It is easy to comprehend why this issue is so emotionally charged and continues to be one of debate and dialog both at the governmental level in political and religious circles.

Judge Bullen Panchol arguably stressed that, it's really isn't rational to consider a law or the attempt by lawmakers to frame this issue into legislation as moral or immoral. In our representative form of government, those who would make laws have clear cut guidelines on how they will decide what will or will not become the law of the land.

The top-level criteria for what become a law in this country is the will of the people. This can be difficult to determine especially in an issue that has fervent believers on both sides. The will of the people is not the sole criteria for a law as the electorate may not be aware of the legal grounds for a law or of the precedent in legal systems that were the background for our system of government. Again, reasons can be found in legal precedent that could be used to justify the legalisation of the death penalty or the banning of it.

Finally, law makers will turn to the consideration of the efficiency of a system of justice and in doing so try to determine if the death penalty is effective especially for children abductors and cattle rustlers in Jonglei State. Although, there are almost as many studies to show that the death penalty does not reduce crime as show the opposite. It is similarly difficult to prove the executing criminals saves lives compared to life in prison. But no matter what side of the issue we come down on, there is no question that this will be an ongoing debate in society for decades to come.

South Sudan's Legal Status of Identity Theft Cases

The law is not a stagnant thing. It is constantly changing, evolving and adapting to new situations and new crimes that must be identified and understood so appropriate laws can be passed to protect honest people from the dishonest ones in South Sudan. This can be a tricky process, especially in this age when crimes using the internet make detection and evidence so difficult but early introduction of such laws in South Sudan can make people behave well and adapt careful consideration while the country is still young and emerging into digital world.

Identity theft is a perfect example of a crime that should be aggressively attacked from the legal community. But because it is a crime that is always changing and adapting, it is sometimes difficult for the legal community to get a firm definition of what identity theft is and particularly how to codify it into a system of laws that can be used to effectively stop it.

Probably the biggest problem with enforcing laws that will lead to the conviction of identity thieves is to develop ways to keep the evidence long enough to seek a conviction. Until we can give law enforcement sufficient tools both to identify and capture identity theft criminals and then to gather sufficient evidence to get a conviction, identity theft will continue to be an allusive enemy in South Sudan because the system is so corrupt.

Unlike a murder where there is a weapon and corpse or cattle rustling where there are physical forms of evidence, much of the footprint of identity theft occurs in cyberspace where there are few fingerprints and tracing the path of the criminal is difficult at best. In that way, tracking down identity thieves resembles the problems legal experts have in defining and then tracking down cyber stalkers or pornography merchants who can be so elusive in an online world.

Consumers who are hit with identity theft face two challenges. One is to stop the continued stealing by thieves who can continue to do their damage even after the crime has been identified. The other is to find the criminals and make it stop. Consumers are frustrated because law enforcement hits roadblocks in their investigations of identity theft cases when they get bribes. But law enforcement professionals are also frustrated because those who might have the evidence they need to capture, prosecute and convict identity thieves often no longer have that evidence that is desperately needed to stop this unique 21st century crime.

In order to give law enforcement what they need, companies that sell consumer data must be regulated more closely and tightly. One big hole in the legal system which favours identity thieves and puts consumers at a disadvantage is that businesses that resell consumer data do not have to notify consumers when their data is being passed along to another agency. Therefore, once a consumer provides his or her private data to a company, that data can be packaged and resold without restriction to as many buyers who care to line up to buy it and the consumer has no idea this is going on.

So, this is a level of consumer protection that can be addressed legally by requiring any company that collects buyer information must be required to notify consumers when that data is being sold and who they are selling it to. If every consumer can retain a complete trail of who is getting their private information, that would empower the private sector to partner with the legal community to put a stop to this level of crime.

If further laws could be improved to require longer retention of transactions of this nature and open access of those records to law enforcement, we would be giving our legal system the weapons they need to stop this crime. And that would be a step forward for all of society to make South Sudan, the cyber world included, a safer place for all of us.

South Sudan Most Feared Government Institution: The NSS!

To even mention the name of this government institution can set off waves of anxiety and stories of abuse and persecution that is unheard of for virtually any other governmental body in this country. It's really amazing the ability of three little words to in-still fear in the hearts of South Sudanese citizen when those three little words are the National Security Service (NSS).

When we look a little closer at the mission of the NSS and their actual record of how they handle most of their cases, the level of hysteria we get ourselves into is really pretty silly and scary one. For the most part, the abuses and draconian methods that we think of when we talk about the NSS are urban myth. You would think that the NSS existed solely to imprison, abduct or kill South Sudanese people, take all of their property and make our lives miserable either through investigations that resemble the Spanish Inquisition or by keeping us all in constant terror.

This is not to say that over the decade, there have not been some abuses that have earned the NSS as least some of the reputation, it's still working to live down. Yes, you can dig back and find some pretty awful abuses that the NSS has committed against citizens in the name of protecting national interest. But to be fair, we can find abuses in many governmental bodies, particularly those with a mission to carry out that is undercover or violent. We can think of phenomenal stories of violence and unethical behaviour by the SPLA, The police, The NSS and all branches of the military. But we don't as a population cringe in terror in talking about those governmental bodies the way we do when the subject of the NSS comes up in conversation.

You have to wonder why the NSS strikes such fear into our hearts. Part of it is the influence of the social media, Facebook and Twitter. The NSS makes a big target and many times the role of an NSS agent is depicted in movies as a heartless mercenary out to take away everything you own including your precious life. The spectre of NSS investigations is feared with the same loathing of a root canal or torture by foreign spies.

But much of it may come from just a plain and simple distain for social media posting. We just don't like the idea of the government taking our precious souls. The cure for this, is to step back and examine why critics are necessary and understand that writing for the operation of a governmental system is the responsibility of all of us. It is not only the patriotic thing to do but it is part of what being a citizen of a great nation does. The NSS are just the clerks assigned with the difficult task of making sure everybody respects nation's national security. And, after all, the system is only fair if everybody is respected and treated like a citizen.

The truth is that the NSS does all it can not to have to resort to drastic measures to help each citizen participate in the support of the government equally. Many times, even the dreaded NSS is really no more painful or difficult than getting a bill from your electric generation company.

It really isn't the NSS fault that the national security laws are complicated and hard to figure out. If we want to fix that, we should go to our parliamentarians and elected officials. The NSS is really in the same boat we are in but just got controlled by crocks Myth Ke Baai in J-ONE to protect ONLY one person out of 13 million - the president, Salva Kiir. They have to figure out the NSS laws and then see to it that we live within them. Blaming the NSS because we don't like the NSS laws or abiding by NSS in general is the old bad news, kill the messenger syndrome.

If we take a more reasonable view of what the NSS is and that they are doing their best, as we all are, to get a job done that not very many people like, we might not only stop fearing and despising them, we might see them as just another governmental body that has to be there just like the military at the federal level, state level and the garbage man or the school board chairman at the local level. Some NSS men are just good honest South

Sudanese doing their best to make the system work, others are so cruel crocks even to their immediate family members. And if we work together, it can work, and we can find ways to make it better.

South Sudan's Consumer Rights and Protection: Alier Gaar Law Firm

The stories in the last few years have included some pretty alarming stories about bad products that have come to South Sudan from China, Uganda, Kenya, Ethiopia and Sudan. And we South Sudanese in the west do look with disgust at failures of a government to assure that products produced by merchants are safe for consumers. This is because our government in countries like Australia maintains a high level of control, testing, and monitoring of products to assure that the consumers of these products are protected, and consumers can buy them with confidence.

Of course, this is not to say that problems with consumer protection have been eliminated. But when a product is found to be unsafe, we have a sophisticated system of recalls and alerts that go out over our media. In this way, that the damage and danger from inferior product is vastly minimised from what it might have been.

Before Judge Bullen Panchol's passing, we had an excellent conversation over the phone, and we exchanged many great insights about laws governing consumer health and consumer rights. He excellently asserted that consumer rights and protection are an important area of focus for manufacturers and merchants in South Sudan, but they are not implemented, he stressed it. These laws have a high level of importance for merchants and that drives up quality control and inspection even before the government or legal systems get involved. That is because the outcome of a recall or product failure, especially if that failure leads to injury or death of a consumer, can be devastating both to the individual merchant or company involved and to the market it serves that placing a high priority on quality is as much about market survival as it is about ethical behaviour by companies.

Today in South Sudan, what can we as consumers expect in the way of our rights and the protections we deserve as being part of this economy? It breaks down to what we consider to be the basics of the contract that is implied when we give someone money for a product or service:

- South Sudanese expect to be able to use the goods safely with no possibility of immediate harm or long-term illness as result of using the product.
- South Sudanese expect the product to perform according to reasonable expectations based on what the product was promoted to do both on the package and in advertisements.
- South Sudanese expect to pay what the product is advertised to cost. We do not accept changes in price after that price is advertised or surprise costs to be added on that we weren't expecting.
- If a product fails to deliver the service it was advertised to deliver, or is found to be flawed in any way, we expect the merchant to refund or replace the product promptly and courteously.
- In the case of food, medicines or other consumables, a South Sudanese expect the product to be made of the highest levels of quality and to be reasonably fresh and usable.
- South Sudanese expect the merchants involved in the sale of the product to stand behind the product with guarantees from the retail merchant all the way to the manufacturer.

South Sudan have not come up with this list of rights and protections on our own products or imports/exports. These are the minimum standards that should be prescribe by our laws to assure that the consuming public can trade with merchant in any kind of product and service and be treated with the same minimum levels of professionalism and quality assurance.

From the merchant's point of view, you might think these high standards of consumer rights and protections would be a burden. But in fact, these laws protect both the consumer and the merchant. That is because these laws make it possible for the buying public to engage in commerce with any merchant that is authorised to do business with confidence.

Consumer protection laws make an active marketplace possible which benefits both consumers and merchants equally. So, complying with consumer protection laws is not just essential from a legal point of view. It makes good sense for merchants to comply fully and perform above expectations in terms of their ability to deliver quality product to their customers in the country. It just makes good business sense and sense of confidence in buying.

South Sudan: Acknowledging Assistance on Legal Divorce and Family Law

For every state, the family and divorce law differ although information that should be given in this section tackles majorly of what is present in every state and how it is dealt with in general. In order to seek a clearer vision regarding a particular topic, you can consult a divorce or family lawyer regarding your status of getting professional advice.

Family is one of the most important units within the society that gives meaning to life. However, when balance is moved, there are matters that needs to be discussed and people who are seeking for advice can be given certain ideas on how the law that governs the family works, some of which are about the totality of marriage, divorce, child custody and child support.

South Sudan Law on Marriage

Laws regarding marriage status in South Sudan are strictly governed by the customary law of the state. However, there are federal regulations that rely on the marital status of the couple in order to determine the federal benefits and rights which invoke the important definition of marriage to the law. Furthermore, the constitution ensures that South Sudan Supreme Court will be able to review the laws which are related to marriage.

Judge Bullen Panchol's Law on Divorce

Agreement on divorce is similar to agreement on separation, marital agreement, and agreement on the settlement of properties which are legally acceptable with the contract settling matters should be introduce and involve. It will not be referred to as an agreement on being divorced because only the court can grant such request. If both parties will fail in reaching the agreement, the case will undergo trial and the decision of the court will be altered. Whatever the court has raised can be modified and will be based on the change in substance and circumstance. Agreements, therefore, can be modifiable or non-modifiable.

Judge Bullen Panchol's agreements settle certain issues that relate to the following should be introduced in Legal System: Alier Gaar Law Firm:

1. Health, life insurance and alimony

2. Division on liabilities and assets

3. Physical and legal custody, visitation, college fund, child support and medical expenses and insurance

Judge Bullen Panchol's Law on Child Custody: Alier Gaar Law Firm

Generally, ordinances authorise courts of having responsibility or jurisdiction of proceedings regarding divorce in order to determine who should have the children's custody under the marriage. Within the common provision, parents of a child who is legitimate are considered as joint guardians of the child and each parent's rights are equal which means that each parent has the right for the child's custody the moment they separate. And because of the controversial authority to decide custody based on the court's jurisdiction, laws within this field are based on the state and traditional customary law.

Judge Bullen's Law on Child Support Need Introduce: Alier Gaar Law Firm

In cases where there is judgment for dissolution, separation, or annulment, the court usually orders that both parents should pay the amount necessary for the child to be supported until proclaimed stable or when the child reached age of independency. Financial support of the child will be based on the facts of the couple's separate cases. The court has the right to consider that both parents are responsible and obliged for supporting the child.

Considerations will be made upon establishment of the amount that should be supported and it will be given to both parents which, under the legal assistance, should provide proper support and proper welfare for the minor including the child's needs.

Judge Bullen Panchol's Legal Assistance and Domestic Violence: Alier Gaar Law Firm

Did you know that many people suffer from domestic violence in South Sudan? Survivors of domestic violence often complain about essential hypertension, migraines, insomnia, chronic pain, depression, anxiety, excessive fatigue, and many others. If you're a victim of domestic violence, you need to seek legal assistant at once.

The body is designed to react with threats coming from the surroundings. You can either fight against the threat or you shy away from it. Individuals react differently when they are threatened and if you're a victim of domestic violence, you can seek the proper legal help so that you will know what to do.

If you don't face this problem, you will end up with the conditions mentioned earlier and you will be under chronic stress. This is not an ideal situation and by opening yourself to professional and expert legal assistant, you will know what to do.

Firstly, you need to report your situation to the concerned agencies; that way, you will receive appropriate assistance. Lots of individuals don't want to report their situation because they are scared but if you're one of them, you should not have second thoughts in fighting against domestic violence.

You can start searching through the list of lawyers in the country. Just ensure that you're looking in the right list. You see, lawyers have different specialisations. In your case, you have to look for a lawyer that specialises in domestic violence. If you can't afford to hire a personal lawyer, you can check with charitable organisations in your local area that can help you in locating pro bono attorneys or lawyers. When you say pro bono, the services of the lawyers are given for free. The charitable organisations can assist you with your case. Once you have a pro bono lawyer, you and your lawyer can now start handling the domestic violence case.

You need to provide all the required details related to the case to your lawyer. Don't try to hide even the smallest detail because this can affect the case in the future. You and your lawyer should trust each other. You should be honest at all times. Once you've developed trust for your lawyer, you will be more comfortable in his or her presence. The lawyer can also give you some advice or may be able to refer you to some counselling services.

Indeed, victims of domestic violence in South Sudan can be terribly affected especially their personal lives. Some victims find it hard to recover from the pains and hurtful memories of domestic violence. Through counselling services, the victims can adjust to their new life and learn to move on. After some time, they will be able to live normal lives again without having any feelings of insecurity, anxiety, or depression.

Domestic violence is not new especially in today's South Sudan modern times. Victims are encouraged to speak out and seek the necessary legal assistant. Whether you're rich or poor, you should not hesitate to seek legal help if you're a victim of domestic violence. Let the person responsible for your sufferings pay for everything. You can get your personal lawyer, or you can ask help from charitable organisations to provide you with a pro bono lawyer.

This is your ticket to start a new life. Be strong and don't lose hope. You're not alone in the battle and with the right legal assistance, you can make it through.

Considering other Legal Assistant Types that Judge Bullen's Law Firm: Alier Gaar Law Firm Recommended

Aside from laws regarding business audit, marriage, divorce, murder, etc., there are still other points wherein legal help matters. The nature of your problem can be attested by other kinds of legal assist which are stated below:

1. Community Unions

This should be able to provide you with a free and legal representation with different kinds of problems in which you are concerned with, and that doesn't only cover issues related to community. Community unions representation that are free can be sought as a more suitable choice that the accepted Legal representation due to the fact that you don't have to assert any kind of contribution, financially, to get legal aid from your chosen union.

2. Law Firms

These are areas of South Sudan wherein law firms are entitled to give free legal aid or advice. These firms tend to specialise in different areas of specificity like employment, government assistant, housing, and immigration cases. A law firm has the option to take in cases wherein legal aid is not entirely available although, these firms may also require a written statement or contract in order to provide the legal help expected of them.

The Fallen Distinguished Judge: The Constitutional Laws Fundamentalist

3. Lawyers on Fixed Fee Interview

There are attorneys or solicitors that provide parts of legal advice only for a fixed or pre-agreed fee. However, there are schemes that tend to offer a fixed amount for free advice. This is beneficial to know if the case you have at hand is worth pursuing or defending in court or would it be just another burden where you can never win. What's good about a fixed interview is that the scheme of equal fee is applicable for everyone whatever the inquiry may be or not considering the income that you have.

4. UN Organisations for motoring

Organisations that are built upon motoring can also provide cheap or even free legal advice or legal service only if you are recognised as a member of their organisation.

5. South Sudan Need Legal insurance

There are no legal insurance companies that render policies wherein it covers the expenses of specific legal aspects like personal injuries, motoring offenses, consumer or client disputes, and problems regarding employment. More importantly, you have to carefully consider the policy if you had one that the company offers. There might be policies that tend to exclude certain legal expenses and may not be able to meet the overall cost of the case.

Juba might have some organisations which might tend to offer legal advice if you pay a price for subscription. There are few businesses or organisations that you can run to when you have difficulties or concerns over your matters, they can make it to the media.

Judge Bullen Panchol's Alier Gaar Legal Assistant and Real Estate Law

Have you ever encountered problems related to real estate or land in South Sudan? Sometimes, no matter how hard you try to avoid having a real estate problem, they just come and you're uncertain about handling legal matters. You should be aware of the different laws and your rights as well as a property owner. You will need the proper legal assistant to deal with real estate and land matters, this was one of Judge Bullen's aspiration to protect citizens from men in public sector grabbing every land in the country.

For instance, you have problems like property contracts, mortgage or lease, and other real property concerns; in this case, you will be dealing with legal matters which an ordinary individual like yourself might find it difficult to understand. You have to look for the best and most reputable attorney in your state or in Juba so that you can handle all the legal matters smoothly. Working with a good attorney will surely cost you so you should know how to maximise the time spent during your consultations and discussions.

Here are the things that you need to keep in mind if you have an appointment with your attorney:

1. Treat your appointment as a serious business meeting. Make sure that you wear the right kind of clothes which show self-confidence and responsibility. You must provide all the needed information to your attorney so that you will be more comfortable dealing with each other. Make sure that the attorney speaks first before you do and try to bring important documents related to the case.

2. You must provide the attorney only with the true facts and information of the case. You have to be honest and make sure that you don't hide anything from your attorney because this can cause future problems. That way, your attorney will also be more open and honest to you about your real estate problem. The attorney should be able to tell you about your options and everything should be clear to you.

3. Once the attorney accepts your real estate problem, you should be aware about the costs it will involve. The attorney might give you a legal services or written agreement. You can also ask the attorney frankly about the fees involve so that there'll be no surprises in the future. Both you and the attorney should be committed to the case to ensure success.

Those are the things that you have to do once you meet with your chosen attorney or lawyer. Remember that it's just an initial consultation and the decision to take the case or not will depend on the attorney. At this first meeting, you should be able to establish trust and good relationship with the legal attorney so that he or she will take the case.

There are so many young lawyers in South Sudan, specially Juba now and other states. By checking the directory of South Sudan attorneys, you will find a reputable attorney which specialises in real estate who lives in your locality. It's a good idea if your attorney lives in your locality because you can easily make an appointment.

So, if you encounter any real estate problem, get a real estate lawyer or attorney. Don't forget to check the background of the attorney and how much real estate cases he or she handled in the past. Be very careful, there are many grievances and disputes which are unsettle in South Sudan's real estate industry. It's young market with a lot of grabbing, corruption and event murdering. Don't just buy any advertise land or property, make proper real estate appraisal or first seek legal assistant. You're going to pay real good money for the lawyer's services so he or she should be the best in your area and help you settle your real estate problems, judge Bullen Panchol advised.

South Sudan Medical Malpractice Laws Need Scrutiny: Judge Bullen's Alier Gaar Law Firm

When you are wrongly misdiagnosed, injured, prescribed with wrong medication, getting a legal claim filed is not always the first thing on your mind in South Sudan. But this is one area that it seems the lawyers descend like vultures on anyone who is injured in any way at all in countries like Australia. This is one way that the legal profession gets such a bad reputation in Western World. Seeing all of those ambulance runners and lawyers trying to talk people into filing malpractice claims on television is not a dignified way to portray any profession.

This whole area of medical malpractice can be pretty confusing to those who are outside of both the legal and the medical professions. But in a strict sense of the word, it may be something looking into if there is a clear case where a doctor either did not do their job or did it so poorly that it caused you additional pain and suffering or injury.

In that kind of situation, you may incur lots of additional medical expenses getting qualified assistant from an injury caused by a doctor who just didn't do his or her job right. So it seems only right that medical malpractice laws would be there to protect citizens from being victimised by doctors who were not doing their best to make you better.

The problem is, when it comes to using the medical malpractice laws to seek some satisfaction for a bad medical situation, it can get quite confusing in South Sudan where those laws are violated on everyday bases by unregulated clinics in healthcare environment. The first thing that might help get some definition of what constitutes medical malpractice is to understand the categories. There are five general types of medical error or medical malfeasance that can throw your case into the category of malpractice. It might be medical malpractice:

- If the doctor is not able to diagnose your illness or does so incorrectly.
- If the doctor or medical facility is too slow in providing medical care resulting in further medical problems for you.
- If the doctor fails to perform a medical procedure that is what you need to recover from injury or illness.
- If mistakes were made in prescribing the right medication or prescribing medication that is harmful to you.
- If the doctor fails to explain what needs to be done or is negligent in warning you of negative side effects of your treatment.

If you have suffered any kind of negative outcome that is directly related to your medical treatment on top of your original problem, it's not too hard to fit what happened to you into this category. If you are a genuine victim of medical malpractice, identifying that is not always the most difficult part of the problem though. The most difficult part may be deciding what to do about it in difficult environment like South Sudan.

This is where that ambulance runner aspect of the legal profession can be as much trouble as they can be of help. To make a decision about whether the potential outcome of a malpractice suit is worth the effort, you need a non-biased viewpoint and advice based on the extent of your grievance and injury and how much you need the resolution to continue your recovery. When a lawyer or law firm pursues you so relentlessly to get a malpractice lawsuit going or they advertise to get that kind of business, you get the idea they are not looking after your best interest but their own. Get a best advice from researching around.

Whatever they try to tell you, malpractice legal actions are not as easy to win as they might seem especially when South Sudan government is not serious in healthcare strict regulation. There are a lot of burdens or proof. So, if you feel you have a case, the best thing is to work with legal advisors whom you trust and know they are not going to guide you to an action that is not in your best interest. Sometimes just using that lawyer to negotiate a resolution with the doctor is the best way to go.

Judge Bullen's Passing Ended Commercial Private Practice: Alier Gaar Law Firm PTY LTD

When Justice Bullen Panchol resigned from judiciary in September 2018. He went further and founded Alier Gaar Law Firm with its offices in Juba and Bor Town with assistance from his children who are working in Juba. He retired into private commercial practice and his work was including advising a broad scope of clients, ranging from large multi-national companies to individuals businesses, in the areas of: asset protection, business structuring arrangements including trusts, partnerships and joint ventures, financial services compliance, intellectual property licensing and trademarks, mergers and acquisitions, family domestic laws, criminal laws and many more consultative services.

As a distinguished judge and law fundamentalist with wealth of legal expertise, experience, and his commitment approaches to many clients was an evident in the tailored, strategic advice and services that he offers. He was very successful in resolving cases through mediation, offers of compromises and settlements, but he also has a solid history of litigation successes. Since the inception of his law firm operation in 2019, there had been overwhelming ques for his expertise seeking specialise advice service. His law commercial acumen includes a working knowledge of business laws, legal tools and methodologies required to collect and analyse data and synthesize this data into reports of significance evident which allow his firm to make operational and strategic decisions based on business legal matters that could contribute to better law practice in South Sudan.

Justice Bullen Panchol underwent a period where he needed to make a decision on future expansion of his law firm while improving efficiency and incorporating lean principles. His challenge was to develop an in-depth cost benefit and risk analysis to identify long term commercial viability and security risks associated with business operation. He was contemplating to perform marketing analysis in order to develop strategies and techniques to promote his private law practice and develop strong metrics to monitor his progress in his strategic growth in the future. This trend was cut short by his passing, his clientele base at his consulting practice was evident that the country is suffering from deficiency of leadership from all arms of government with leadership malpractices everywhere.

CHAPTER FIVE
GETTING PERSONAL: JUSTICE BULLEN PANCHOL AS A FAMILY MAN TILL HIS FINAL MOMENTS.

Bullen Panchol was a man with a large family. Although he lived more than half of his life fighting for the autonomous, independent, and developed South Sudan, he never for once lacked in playing his role as a father. Bullen Panchol's family was rather a large one, he was blessed with twelve (12) daughters and nine (9) sons, with his eldest son as Martin Alier 'Marto' Panchol is now late. He passed shortly after the death of his Baba Bullen. Even though he had a large family of twenty-one children, he valued education and ensured all his children had the best education they can attain. He never distinguished between any of his children, he taught togetherness and nourished the orientation of living in a harmonious and uniting family. Justice Bullen Panchol married not just one wife, but he ensured his home was a home of love as there was no disparity between his children. Although all twenty-one (21) children were not from the same mother, he showed them affection and instilled quality integrity in all children.

Growing up as a family, they lived most of their lives both in South Sudan and Kenya especially during the war. Bullen Panchol got married to late Ayak Benjamin Agok Guor during his life as a barrister and had children and later in mid 1985 married to Aluel Biar Deng-aguek, his second wife. However, due to the rising chaos in South Sudan, his family had to emigrate to Ethiopa, then back forth to South Sudan and moved as far as to Kenya for safer haven. Before that, his first son was already in Kenya for his secondary education.

Although Justice Bulllen spent lots of his early years fighting for his country and at the same time catering for his family during tough times of liberation struggles. Before Justice Bullen Panchol moved his whole family to Kenya, his first son Martin Alier was schooling in one of the renowned primary school in Eldoret Kenya. After successfully moving his family to an assured safety, Justice Bullen travelled back to South Sudan to continue in his position as judge and as a soldier. His ideal and morals for upbringing was evident in the impact some of his children are making, representing South Sudan within and outside the country.

One would not be wrong to say as much as he strived for the unity of South Sudan, his family was a reflection of the harmony he wished for South Sudan. Being a scholar himself, he ensured all his children earned a formal degree, in which out of twenty-one children, eight of them are university graduates. During his lifetime, he met six of his grandchildren. Let's get introduced to The Panchols families and children.

Justice Bullen Panchol's Family Composition and Social Status: Wives, Partners and Children.

1st Wife Late Ayak Agok Guor Family

First wife late Ayak Benjamin Agok Guor Malek hailed from Pakeer clan, Hol - Ajang Majok section of Twic East County, Jonglei State.

Children of Late Ayak Benjamin Agok Guor

- Martin Alier Bullen Panchol Awal – son (Deceased on 16th May 2020).
- Susan Nyiel Bullen Panchol Awal – daughter (Married to Eng. Deng Diar Diing from Kongor, Twic East County and has three children.
- Marina Anyich Bullen Panchol Awal – daughter.
- Apiu Bullen Panchol Awal – daughter.

- Agok Bullen Panchol Awal – son (Deceased).
- Asara Bullen Panchol Awal – daughter.
- Diing Bullen Panchol Awal – daughter.
- Abeny-dit Bullen Panchol Awal – daughter (Deceased).
- Ayen Bullen Panchol Awal – daughter.

2nd Wife Aluel Biar Deng-aguek

Aluel Biar Deng-aguek, hails from Jalle, Juet, Jaak section, Bor County of Jonglei State.

Aluel's Children

- Samuel Ayuen Bullen Panchol Awal – son (Married to Yar Ateny Majok with one child).
- Lian Bullen Panchol Awal – daughter (Deceased).
- Nyiel (Toto) Bullen Panchol Awal – daughter.
- Kut Bullen Panchol Awal – son.
- Mary Anyich Bullen Panchol Awal – daughter.
- Awak Bullen Panchol Awal – daughter.

3rd Wife Yar Ageer Arok

Yar Ageer Arok hails from Ajuong clan, Nyapiny section of Twic East County, Jonglei State.

Yar's Children

- William Alier Bullen Panchol Awal – son.
- Awal Bullen Panchol Awal – son.
- Abraham Tiir Bullen Panchol Awal – son.

Mrs Karama Awad

Mrs Karama Awad, hails from Moro tribe of Western Equatoria State and is the mother of Tiir-dit Bullen Panchol Awal – son, (Tiir is married with two children).

Mrs Anek Makueng

Mrs Anek Makueng, hails from Agaar, Rumbek section of Lake State and is the mother of Abeny-thii Bullen Panchol Awal – daughter.

Mrs Mary Alich

Mrs Mary Alich, hails from Gogrial, Awan Mou section of Warrap State and is the mother of Jooh Bullen Panchol Awal – son.

His Marriage with Ayak Benjamin Agok Guor

Justice Bullen Panchol got married to Ayak Benjamin Agok Guor in his early years as a Barrister at Sudan's judiciary. Before going to the bush to become a freedom fighter fighting for the autonomous state of South Sudan. Justice Bullen Panchol engaged in marital rites with his first wife and gave birth to his daughter Susan Bullen Panchol and first-born son Martin Alier Panchol (now late). She ensured she did her best to take care of the family while her husband was in the battlefields ensuring the future of South Sudan and most importantly the future of his offspring, not saddled with crimes, war, genocide, and many other pestilences he experienced while growing up.

His First-born Son Martin (Marto) Alier Bullen Panchol

Martin Alier Panchol was a man of jovial acts and witty and funny sarcasm. He was born in South Sudan but schooled and lived most of his life in Kenya. His schooling was in Kenya where he lived with his uncle till, he changed schools and his father, and the rest of his family relocated to Kenya following the unrest in South Sudan. He experienced the emotion of living with his family once again. Late Martin Alier Panchol was a man of great taste and a fan of living his best life while he still breathes, he wore designers, partied hard, and was a friend to many. In life, everyone hopes to live until they are old and grey. However, that was not the case for Martin Alier as he suffered from the rarest type of diabetes, which was detected and treatment rather too late. He slumped into his last sleep and woke up no more days after he heard the news of his father's death.

Second Son Ayuen Bullen Panchol

Known for his interest in private business and shaping his country through innovative ideas, he took over his father's intellect strengths and noble integrity. He graduated from Kenya Methodist University (KEMU) with bachelor's degree in Business Administration. He runs his Forex Exchange business in Juba, South Sudan. He is married to Yar Ateny and they have a one-year old daughter together.

Kut Bullen Panchol

Final Year University Student in Business Administration in Kenya, a promising young ambitious gentleman who promises his father a lot of goodies to make his name shine.

Bullen Panchol Daughters

Justice Bullen Panchol was blessed with ten beautiful daughters. In no particular order, below are short introductions of the ten beautiful ladies.

Susan 'Suzy' Bullen Panchol

The eldest daughter of the Panchol family. She was once a journalist at the citizen media group before resigning to be a researcher at Global Communities and became a full-time mother. She graduates with bachelor's degree in mass communication and master's degree in Developmental Studies. Married to Eng. Deng Diar Diing Manyok in 2015, she lives in Kenya with her husband and their three children.

Asara Bullen Panchol

Definition of beauty with brains. In 2019, she won Miss South Sudan and also ran for the international Miss Earth pageantry in 2019 and became Miss Earth South Sudan. She is also beauty and peace ambassador for ROSS. She studied at Kenya Methodist University and graduated with degree in Mass Communication, Media and Journalism to earn her a career as Communication and Liaison Coordinator at Chemonics International Incorporation. She is also an advocate against the pollution of the earth. She has been featured in a number of campaigns against pollution, an example is the #solutionnotpollution social campaign. She has also represented South Sudan in other countries creating awareness of the beauty of the country in spite of the public perception of the country.

Apiu Bullen Panchol

One of Panchol's highly outspoken person, she has great character of judge Bullen Panchol and shared a lot in common. She graduated from Kenya Methodist University Class of 2014 in Nairobi, Kenya. Full of life and always there for her siblings. She works at Qatar National Bank.

Avena Diing Bullen Panchol (Laboni Bullen)

Avena is an astonishing young ambitious professional. She is quite industrial and has an entrepreneurial mindset. A graduate of International Relations and Diplomacy from the Kenya Methodist University. She works as aviation consultant with South Sudan's international airlines companies.

Ayen Bullen Panchol (Dolly Bullen)

Currently studying at Kenya Methodist University although she spent some months studying at the Technical University Mombasa, Kenya. She is a student studying undergrad degree in logistic and supply chain.

Marina Anyich Bullen Panchol

Marina is Judge Bullen's second oldest charming daughter currently working in Juba, South Sudan. She studied banking and finance at the African Nazarene University and currently works with the United Nations World Food Program in South Sudan. One can see the humanitarian attribute Justice Bullen instilled in almost all of his children.

Mary Anyich Bullen Panchol

She won a scholarship to study in Canada by the World University Service of Canada. She currently lives and studies at St. Francis Xavier University, pursuing Bachelor of Science majoring in Nursing.

Priscilla Nyiel Bullen Panchol

Currently studying International Development at St. Francis Xavier University Canada but lives in Antigonish Nova Scotia. She takes after her father, as she is an advocate for gender equality, a better life for refugees, and a less vulnerable society habitable for the old and young people of South Sudan. She has also represented South Sudan in varying capacities particularly in summit related to refugee awareness.

Other names of his children include Abeny, Awal, Tiir and Jooh Bullen Panchol, Kut Bullen, William Alier Bullen Panchol, Awak Bullen Panchol, and others.

Justice Bullen Panchol Awal and His Grand Children

Every father hopes and prays to be a grandfather and give his blessings to his grandchildren before they ascend to the heavens. Justice Bullen

Panchol Awal in his lifetime saw and showed fatherly love to all his six (6) grandchildren. Suzy Nyiel is a mother to two boys and a girl while Ayuen is a father to a one-year-old daughter and Tiir Bullen with two sons. Without a doubt, one would agree that he lived a good life and was blessed with a great life and his children leaves no stone untouched in showing their humanitarian sides in one way or the other.

CHAPTER SIX

ANOTHER LOSS FOR THE PANCHOLS: TRAGIC PASSING OF MARTIN PANCHOL AWAL (ALIER-MARTO).

Martin Bullen Panchol was the kind of man you can find a friend in at the first meet. He was a caring, patriotic, and intelligent man. He was a man for the people, both young and old enjoy his company. A gentleman to the core, quite honest and does not mince words. Martin or 'Marto' as he was often called was the first-born son of Judge Bullen Panchol Awal Alier and Ayak Agok Guor. He was born in the 1979 when Sudan second civil war was ticking bomb, one can only imagine that, it was where Martin got his resilience.

During his early years, Martin did not only aspire to be a future leader, he acted in roles that made it quite evident he possessed the qualities. He clearly understood how important it was to take life as it is and enjoy it the best way one can. Martin had a highly promising and entertaining lifestyle. One would not be wrong when we say he took after the brains of his father as he was a scholar, particularly in the history niche. If you were looking for a person to engage with intellectually with a mix of witty sarcasm sprinkled with some humour, he always had interesting things to say. Each of his friends had funny but interesting nicknames formed by Martin to which many found rather admirable. He was quite a good storyteller as his eloquence and ways he structures his words makes you want to pay rapt attention. As a people's person with an admirable intellect, everyone wanted to associate with him. In a number of ways, Martin had an interesting character, so jovial he could easily create friendships with the young and old. His friends used to tease him that he could make a cool career from being a stand-up comedian as his funny nature makes people want to imitate his comedy characters.

Martin was not one who would back away from challenging environments, as a matter of fact, he finds his way to conquer and adapt to such environment the best way he sees fit. When you hang around Martin, you are sure to have a full dose of laughter as he could be jokingly provocative, and he knows how to do that to ease a tense environment. Justice Bullen Panchol Awal was quite aware of this in his son and how he was a spitting image of his father both in the act and in wits. He recognised his son was intelligent and had potentials, hence why he enrolled him in one of the best elementary schools in mainstream Kenya. While he was a frontline soldier in the war between South Sudan against North Sudan, he cared for the wellbeing and education of his children. In 1997, he took a leave of absence from the SPLA to travel to Kenya to find a better school for Martin, as he was a man who valued quality education. He arrived at Eldoret city in Kenya where his maternal family lived.

Justice Bullen handed Martin over to his maternal uncle Dr. Angok Kuol Tiir, who took care of him and enrolled him into a good school. Justice Panchol travelled back to South Sudan to join the rest of his family and back to his duties in the army. All through his primary education, Martin lived in Eldoret, Kenya with his uncle. His Alma Mata was one of the best schools in Eldoret Central Business District. It took the management and teachers many surprises when they discovered how much of an academic genius, he was at his age in Hills school then. In his first year, he was announced as the second-best student in Primary 7 in the entire province. Martin continued to live in Kenya with his uncle and his family. When he was set to write his Kenyan Certificate for Primary Examinations (KPCE) to make him transition into secondary school in 1998. He wrote and scored a highly topping second position in the whole of Rift Valley Province. His father and uncle were immensely proud of him.

Upon the release of the KPCE result, he was accepted into one of Kenya's National High School for his secondary education. However, he recognised his abilities and turned down that offer, he demanded his father enrolled him into Ruiru High School in Nairobi. Not considered to be a mere school, it is considered to be one of Nairobi's prestigious high school. Ruiru High School was a renowned school that attracted the finest and brightest international students within Africa and from other western countries. His father always wanted the best for his children, hence why he enrolled him into one of the schools considered to be quite expensive, but he had high faith in his son's academic prowess and behaviour development.

To who much is given, much is expected, Justice Bullen encouraged him to focus on his education and leave out other frivolities that may jeopardise his education. Martin was admitted into the boarding house of the prestigious Ruiru High School, an opportunity many South Sudanese teenagers wished they had. Martin did quite well in high school and transitioned excellently with flying colours in his academics. Along with the terms and conditions of boarding schools, Martin was not permitted to leave the school premises till the end of a term except when he was visited or inevitably had to.

After the end of each term when students were released to go home, Martin catches a bus to Eldoret in an eight hours journey to Eldoret. This made him develop impressive skills of leadership and assuming responsibilities early in his life. He makes a single trip every term as all he'll be needing from provisions to upkeep money, and other essentials are all provided to last him a term. He is escorted to the bus school gate and signed in by his uncle. Martin continued to make excel at his education while he transitioned to his form two successfully.

The First Phase of Hope: Martin's Turbulence Dramatic Swift Turnarounds

In mid-2000, the hostility open fires, and escalations had subdued between the old Southern Sudan and Northern Sudan's Khartoum regime. The suppression of hostilities was a gleaming hope of ceasefire and peace reigning in Sudan again. The peace process between north and south Sudan was about to kick-start in Kenya. The halt of hostilities brought about serenity and Judge Bullen was appointed by SPLA commander Dr. John Garang as a high-profile negotiator in designing a peace mechanism and was advised to relocate to Nairobi Kenya.

This provided a golden opportunity for the Bullen Panchol's family, it availed them the chance for their family to live under the same roof. Judge Bullen Panchol travelled to Eldoret, Kenya with the rest of his family to his maternal uncle Dr. Angok. He rented a townhouse not far away from his uncle's residence. He enrolled the rest of his children in schools in Eldoret, Kenya. This reunited Martin with his family as he gets to spend quality time during the holidays to strengthen the bond of family with his siblings.

Upon settling in Eldoret, Kenya, Judge Bullen headed to Nairobi where he was stationed and assigned to prepare the peace process and other national duties. While far away from home, Judge Bullen never failed to fulfill his fatherly duties, he sends financial upkeep to his wife in Eldoret to cater for food and other basic family and home maintenance. His job involves a lot of travels within Kenya and sometimes to Southern Sudan, yet he never neglected his fatherly duties.

In the second term of form two in Martin's high school, he was given the responsibility where he is handled all his school fees to go and deposit in school bank. Martin Alier took this as a golden opportunity to invest in his favourite fashion items. Upon failure to pay school fees and further education administration revealing the act he had committed; he was suspended from Riuru High School and his father was informed about this incident. Without leaving things to chance, Judge Bullen did not hesitate to find him another school based on Martin's recommendation and choice.

The Second Phase of Hope: Martin's Choice of Lifestyle.

Martin was a gentleman of quality, rich, and affluent taste. His choice of restaurants, the choice of the menu he orders are not the regular cheap meals. His sense of fashion suggests he has a fine taste of top-quality fashion items, perfumes, and he is not one to engage in gulping cheap alcohols. What he chooses to wear are recognized designers. He was gifted a gold watch by his father in 2000. The watch was more than an item, it was a gift that denotes a sign of grooming an admirable intelligent young man.

As expected, humans will have their fair share of life's ups and downs. For Martin, he was getting suspended from Riuru High School. It cost Judge Bullen thousands of dollars to ensure his first-born son and only oldest son completed high school. Martin on the other hand had taken so keenly about his lifestyle to a much rather extreme level making each member of his family worried on his behalf. His lifestyle began to plummet terribly as he was taken from one high school to another, without him settling in anything. A typical act of youthful exuberance and he was oblivious of what he needs to do for himself.

This escalated stress level in the family, as their rising star is fast becoming quite dim and he is taken so much time to realise the decline. Martin began to network across East Africa and garnered a huge diverse network of friends and social currency. He became quite popular amongst Kenyan and South Sudanese people. He was quite the life of the party which earned him his nickname/hype-name "MARTO". Judge Bullen never backed out from supporting him, however, Martin's need grew more demanding financially.

Judge Bullen provided all he requested thinking he'd make Martin have a change of heart, but it turned out to be wrong. Martin's appetite for the luxury lifestyle became unquenchable as he wanted to be known as a high class, high taste man. Advice, reprimanding, and other channels were employed to make Martin standout and switch back to be the typical example of a splitting image like his father, all fell on deaf ears. Certain people were convinced he had been bewitched while others clung on the hope of Martin turning a new leaf someday.

Finally, in 2002, Martin finished high school with a rather poor grade in Manor House High School in the town of Kitale Kenya. For someone who has always had commendable results, many people rejected the result of his high school performance in form four. However, because he did not commit to his studies, but was glad he showed interest to sit for his examinations.

The second phase of hope for everyone was seeing his willingness to further his studies in the college. However, Martin's lifestyle suffered no setback as his choice of fashion were flashy, he found solace in alcohol, and he was the 'ladies' men'. This phase was a trembling and tremendously challenging moment as it was much difficult to control a man of his age. He began to slip away so often from his family, he seldom sleeps at home and no one dared question his whereabouts in the family.

All these happened during the absence of Judge Bullen. Even though he enjoyed the exuberant life of his youth, he never lost the respect or love for his immediate family and relations. Whenever he was not under the influence of alcohol, Martin kept his cool. A good number of family members, friends, and well-wishers reached out to convince Martin about such a lifestyle. He gives a listening ear and promises to turn a new leaf, however, upon their departure, he resumes gulping down alcohol at the pub.

Martin's state and lifestyle choice was a challenge for everyone who cared about him. He never backed out from his expensive taste and drinking of alcohol. On a few occasions, he falls ill, he gives promises not to resume his dastardly acts, but the moment he regains good health and strength, he leaves home and comes back a complete wreck. At this moment, the little faith and hope people had for his lifestyle began to fade away.

The Third Phase of Hope

The third phase of hope did not come about not until the comprehensive peace agreement-CPA signed in 2005 between the South and North Sudan in Naivasha, Kenya. The real hope for all South Sudanese was restored by the CPA and the hope for Judge Bullen Panchol's family became brighter. A new rumour came lurking, that Judge Bullen had been appointed to the constitutional court in Khartoum to review the nation's holy document at upcoming Sudan's Government of National Unity. It was later confirmed as a reality from Dr. John Garang.

Another speculation came out that Dr. John Garang had appointed his interim government in the Southern Sudan region under autonomy and should Southern Sudan opted for a separate state after five years according to CPA then Judge Bullen Panchol Awal will be the Chief Justice for autonomy and the then independent Southern Sudan. Huge news that was widely anticipated by those that knew Judge Bullen but for the family it was more of jubilation and joyful time to hear such news.

It was also a hope to see Martin go with his father to Khartoum and live with him for a little while. In Khartoum, alcohol is not sold randomly in any restaurant, it's restricted due to Sharia laws. The hope for Martin to change in Khartoum was based on Khartoum restrictive lifestyle. Martin initially agreed to travel to Khartoum with his father to officially settle there, however, he had a change of heart and insisted he'd rather stay in Kenya with the rest of the family. Being a smart young man, he knew what life in Khartoum will turn out to be, he travelled to Khartoum with less anticipation of better a life. According to Martin and his escapades, Kenya was the best for having the time of your life. Third phase hope had raised the hope and

The Fallen Distinguished Judge: The Constitutional Laws Fundamentalist

kept every family member anticipating for the best, but Judge Bullen continues to have faith that Martin will change someday, he loved his boy beyond description. Whilst Judge Bullen is in Khartoum, he sent family budgets monthly and Martin's share of the budget was always calculated.

In the year 2006, Martin discussed with his father to send money to further his university education. His father was glad he was starting to realize what mattered to his life by requesting for funds to apply for higher learning admissions. Judge Bullen did not hesitate nor probed him, he provided him the money as he was impressed and trusted his son to do right by him. Rather than ignore him based on his recent pattern of behaviours, Judge Bullen asked Martin to assure him of his keenness and choice to further his education.

Martin successfully convinced his father that he was fully prepared to attend university and he meant it. The funds were provided. Upon receiving the money, his true intentions of getting the funds were not for education purposes, he had other plans. This came as a shock to everyone as what his true intentions were revamping his wardrobe, gaining credibility in South Sudan as a young man of high class and taste.

At this moment, it looked like Martin prioritized his appearance and lifestyle more than his future. Yet, he maintained his jovial, easy-to-approach mannerism, a true gentleman. If you happen to meet him at a restaurant and exchange pleasantries, he'd ask you to order anything you want. He is soft-hearted and has got negotiating skills, his sweet smiles and words can be quite a welcome chat buddy.

The Fourth Phase of Hope.

As Martin continues to shake the hope, everyone had in him, his health began to deteriorate. The alcohol had damaged his organs and had begun to show severely damaged on his appearance. Martin was a young, tall, well-built man, but due to his excess indulgence of alcohol, he began to shrink off and his fashions began to shrug off him, a sign of severity alcohol abused.

After trying every approach, they could to salvage his situation to quit drinking, his family, and close friends of his father, everyone threw their hands - a Dinka interpretation of having had enough of something. However, for Judge Bullen and immediate family members, Martin is part of a family and it's our duty to protect him and provided him with support where necessary.

His peers have now moved on with their life path, some are highly successful in their careers, others settled down to have families of their own. Each of them well-educated and scattered all over the world and fulfilling their dreams. However, Martin had chosen to remain the same Martin Alier. Despite all these oddly consequentialisms, no matter how successful all his friends are, they had never overlooked or down looked Martin Panchol. They know him in and out, a man of the people, a man with a pure heart and a never eat alone man.

The Fifth Phase of Hope

The fifth phase of hope for Martin Alier was in 2011. South Sudan became a recognized and separate state from the rest of Sudan. The autonomy and independence that made every man and woman of South Sudanese indigene who were residing in Kenya, Uganda, Ethiopia, and other neighbouring countries relieved and became safe to come home to their motherland.

It was overwhelming jubilation amongst the South Sudanese and brought great hope for Martin to move to the world's newest capital in Juba city. After some months, Martin moved to Juba. Juba was a canvas, void of any infrastructure, so people had to start from scratch. S perfect opportunity for a reborn for Martin.

Martin remained in Juba whilst his father encouraged him to network and navigate, till he is well acquainted with his surroundings and its people. He also encouraged him to visit some government ministries and to leverage on his friend making skills to network and earn a job.

Nevertheless, Judge Bullen continues to monitor Martin with his daily activities, and he showed some bit of development and improvement that has raised some significant hope. Fortunately, Martin was accepted into a job by the Ministry of Interior. A ministry that was concerned with managing the affairs of law and order in the cities across South Sudan including police jurisdictions.

Martin embraced his new job with much seriousness and gave his utmost dedication. He comes home every evening afternoon nicely dressed without signs of substance influence. It seemed that the rebirth of the new South Sudan gave Martin a new purpose in life. He was quite enthusiastic about the future and everyone in the family saw tremendous dreams come true. Everyone in the family saw magnificent dreams come true, a changed everyone has been yearning for.

However, this met an abrupt end. As months go by, Martin became acquainted with the city life and now had conquered every part of Juba. He often slept-in every morning missing out at work. His manager became concerned of his whereabouts every day. Martin has gone back to his former lifestyle, a behaviour that distracted every plan he wanted to achieve.

Perplexed and shocked by his recent behaviour, his family and friends became worried. Now, he has no job due to his lack of commitment. Years continues to move by, and Martin's case grew worse. His younger siblings started to graduate from universities. Martin's health began to fail him the more and his appearance could not hide that fact anymore. Judge Bullen and the family relations stepped into Martin's rescue, with any modern treatment available. His health was managed and severely warned by his doctors to maintain a healthy lifestyle and stay clear of alcohol as it may trigger his condition and make it worse. Martin would abstain two to three weeks without alcohol but could not hold it in for a month without barely getting drunk. To some family members, it was like a twisted cast and complex to comprehend but with others, it was just a bad habit grown into lifestyle behaviour.

Devastated and angry that all their attempts had gone into the drain, Judge Bullen Panchol and his loved ones wanted Martin to have a family of his own maybe it will give him a purpose and teach him to be responsible. They proposed he got married and bear children that will be well taken care of. It was quite a challenge for Martin that he ignored the advice for so long. Martin and his vainglorious, he was quite stubborn and did not want to succumb to the family's decision over his.

In early 2019, Martin's health grew worse, his BMI does not correspond with his physique. He often felt tired and was often at his weakest. His father and the entire family took charge to transported Martin for further health assessment in India. While no one understood his optimal weight and overall health challenges, the family was worried that Martin's wellbeing is no more in great shape. Upon arriving in New Delhi, India, he was rushed to emergency for full blood counts test and sugar glucose level tests. After a couple of hours, Martin's medical examination results came out positive to lifestyle diabetes, the last stage of diabetes type IV. He was literally in the last stage of dying, the doctors warned the family.

Martin's treatment remedies included adjusting nutritional diets and zero consumption of substances and prohibiting alcohol intakes. After a few weeks of staying in India, his health improved. His family decided to take him back home in Juba, South Sudan with stern advice from the doctors to be adhered to.

While back home in Juba, South Sudan, Martin was placed on strict monitoring mechanism diets and regular prohibited of random hanging out with friends but again given Martin's age, you cannot fully control a fully grown gentleman, so the family still give him some time to mingle with some of his friends. This was done to preserve little life for him since health practitioners warned severally.

The Double Shocking Phase: The Passing

On Wednesday, May 13th, 2020 at 20:30 East African Time, known as the darkest day in South Sudan. Judge Bullen Panchol Awal gave up the ghost and was pronounced dead. His death was the most demeaning thing nature could do to a country that needed such skilful all-time judge. Judge Bullen succumbed to a heart attack that did not even last him three days, he was also diagnosed to suffer from a short strike of pneumonia. His oldest son Martin was severely affected by the sudden passing of his father. Since the passing of his father, Martin refused to drink even a glass of water and completely refused to eat anything for two days.

His family was torn between dealing with the loss of the family pillar, i.e. the passing of Judge Bullen and the deteriorating health situation of Martin Alier. It was a tough and rough time for the mourning family. Little did they know another tragedy was looming. On the 16th of May 2020, while the family was preparing for the funeral service of Judge Bullen Panchol, Martin collapsed in the room and never woke up.

He was rushed to hospital by his younger brother Ayuen Bullen Panchol and his other two cousins, however, it was too late. Sadly, Martin was pronounced dead, the love between the two duos was unbreakable (Judge Bullen and his son, Martin). While growing up, our fathers, whether for good or ill, are our earliest and strongest examples of manliness.

Even for those who never had their father, his influence is a major one, conspicuous for its absence. It is therefore only natural that the death of a man's father is an event that holds incredible and often very painful significance. This is what Martin Alier could not cope with - the death of his father. Being diabetic (rarest TYPE IV) patient, you cannot fast for a few hours let alone days. Hence, Martin's sudden passing was caused by his diabetic condition and the sudden shock of never having to call Baba again because his confidant and supporter, more importantly, Father is no more. The family is very deeply saddened by his demise to the point no one can't even imagine him missing among the Panchols. May his precious soul Rest in Peace.

BOOK PHASE 2 – JUDGE BULLEN PANCHOL'S AMBITION, HARD WORK AND LEGACY.

CHAPTER SEVEN
FULL AUTONOMY OF THE JUDICIARY: BUILDING THE IDEAL LEGAL SYSTEM OF SOUTH SUDAN.

The judicial arm of South Sudan has been in a state of lack of independence and to be frank only little faith is entrusted to this arm of government, because of its anecdotal judgments influenced by corruption and lack of justice. Based on information available, there seems not to be a well-defined code of judicial ethics existing in South Sudan. Before Justice Bullen Panchol's retirement, amidst the corruption and exploitation, not one South Sudanese judge seems to have been sanctioned, disciplined, or impeached, hence making it difficult to assess proceedings under the existing provisions that would follow international standards on the independence of South Sudan's judicial arm. In the case where the minimum guidance of the Judiciary Act offers as regards the composition of the body making decisions on the first occurrence of alleged misconduct as well as the review of disciplinary decisions, hence be insufficient in guaranteeing an independent review.

Concerning the legal profession, the text that formally controls it in South Sudan i.e. the Advocacy Act 2003, was either not implemented or became obsolete. As a result, until new laws are passed, the legal profession in South Sudan will continue to remain in a legal vacuum. One major consequence of this, is the protracted absence of established rules and uniform practices that rules access to the profession. This means individuals are just accorded the title and privileges of being lawyers without applying verifiable criteria to test their competency. The period of completion of the pupillage with a senior lawyer as mandated by Sudanese law although remained maintained even after independence. What remained was that the conditions of access to the legal profession are yet to be applied uniformly. The continuous absence of coherent and clear procedures for admission to the bar hinders the total quality of services provided by the legal profession.

The legal profession in operation presently in South Sudan appears to be largely fragmented between Lawyers with Civil law background who are trained mainly in Arabic in South Sudan, and the other foreign lawyers and legal professionals trained vastly in the diaspora under the 5 legal system. Not until 2012, no functional legal professional association represent the entirety of the legal body in South Sudan today. Now the South Sudan Law Society and South Sudan Bar society are in existence. Also, the issue of creating a unified regulatory framework and body for the legal profession will need a structure and professional culture that brings together legal and linguistic professional backgrounds.

Concerning legal training, postgraduate studies, and bar courses, in all three cases, there are no structures that govern the provision or those provided seem not to function properly, or the provider has insufficient resources. It appears there is no continuing legal education that was available except you went overseas to study further. It is quite obvious that South Sudan lacks a centralized program of legal aid. One improvement is the initiated pro-bono legal aid program that was administered by the Ministry of Justice. However, this initiative seems not to reach those entitled to have legal assistance provided in accordance with international criteria.

South Sudan currently experience legal pluralism as the domestic customary law and other sources of law. Domestic law is the one main source of social order and stability within South Sudan and acts based on decisions in the preponderance of criminal and civil cases. For instance, during the civil war between both parties, customary law was one of the major conflicting factors that stem from the coexisting identities within the borders of the country in which the North dominant group considers themselves Arabs and are Islamic and utilize these elements in determining wealth and power distribution as well as development opportunities. The different concepts and legal systems in South Sudan merged up during the CPA to an extent that it became impossible to differentiate what law originated from the pre-existing judicial culture and that which was as a result of interaction with other legal cultures and interaction with national laws. The procedures of local and national laws infiltrate both up and down South Sudan's judicial hierarchy. For instance, according to Late Judge Bullen Panchol, he argued that, some written laws that most traditional chiefs apply sentences, while some judges apply procedures and principles gotten from local cultures. Hence making the principle of legal certainty thoroughly undermined as it becomes quite hard to know what law is applied in a certain place and a certain case.

The parliament of South Sudan continues to encounter numerous tasks in passing new laws and amending obsolete ones. Between July 2011 and September 2012, 90 laws had been enacted and several others were in the second reading. In the first half of 2013, important laws passed were that of political parties and elections. Despite the remarkable pace of legislation, there was a clear indication of the disparity between the financial and human resources allocated for the day-to-day legislative tasks. Furthermore, some important differences exist between the Judicial Act and the Transitional Constitution pertaining to the rights of the Chief Justice. The rights and power to "grant provisional judicial power to any court judge or person for a certain period and may renew such rights", an authority that had not been set out in the Constitution. Meaningfully, the Judiciary Act also recommends that the Chief Justice is answerable to the Presidency for the administration of the judiciary which is not stated in the Transitional Constitution. This disparity makes it quite difficult to pass judgment without the presidency interference.

The belief of separation of powers is the foundation of an independent and unbiased justice system, Justice Bullen Panchol stressed it. Having high esteem to the legal provisions in place, in South Sudan, the constitutional laws and provisions assure the principle of impartiality and the independence of her judiciary. The law on the judiciary and the Transitional Constitution protects the independence of the judiciary system as an institution, which also safeguards its protection from unnecessary interference. Till today, even with the protection of the Transitional Constitution, the police and other governmental bodies are still yet to respect the principle of the independence of the judiciary.

CHAPTER EIGHT
BETTER LIFE FOR THE GIRL CHILD: EDUCATION EMPOWERMENT AND FIGHT AGAINST UNDERAGE MARRIAGE.

In most developing countries in Africa, Asia, and other Arab countries, girl's underage of eighteen (18) often get married due to incessant pressure from parents, relatives, religious, or cultural rites, and poverty. Many are victims of limited access to quality education and gender bias i.e. parents who favour the male-child rather than seeing both genders as equal and worthy of education.

Other cases are due to limited job opportunities, hence influencing the continuity of the bias and inhumane practice. The emotional, mental, and physical impact child marriage has for child brides in terms of health risk (copulating and giving birth at a young age), making them less independent by reducing earning opportunities. Child marriage does not only put an end to a girl's aspirations and hopes, it robs her of her rights to education and rights to end poverty, as well as achieve economic equity and growth. Putting an end to this paedophilic act masked as a cultural or religious practice is not just the ethically correct thing to do but also the good thing to happen to a country's economy.

According to the analysis of the World Bank Group, the economic cost of child marriage is high. Therefore, putting an end to early child marriage and childbearing can potentially reduce population growth and fertility in the most under-developed country. Another adverse effect is the children whose mothers gave birth to them at a younger age are vulnerable and are at high risk of mortality at age five or are affected by stunted physical development.

Worldwide, the calculated benefits of lower under-five death rates and malnutrition could rise to more than $90 billion yearly by the year 2030.

In South Sudan, the bare minimum legal structure around child marriage is not well-defined. According to UNICEF, 52% of girls of South Sudan are married before they turn 18 and 9% are escorted to their spouse's home before age 15. The Transitional Constitution which became active in operation in 2011 assures women the right to consent to marriage, and penal code provisions criminalize "kidnapping or abducting a woman to compel her to get married". Also, the 2008 Child Act includes provisions planned to protect children under 18 from being forced into marital duties. Based on statistics, out of 10 states in South Sudan, Child marriage is most common in Unity (67% of the women were married off before age 18), Upper Nile and Western Bahr El Ghazal (48%), and Western Equatoria (50%). The conflict in South Sudan contributed to the high rate of early child marriage as most families saw the act as a survival tactic due to a high level of malnutrition, erosion, instability, insecurity, and economic decline.

Primarily, child marriage is influenced heavily by gender inequality and in South Sudan, it is additionally driven by armed conflict, family status, gender norms, and weak legal representation. Females with disabilities are particularly at high risk of being forced into marriage or prostitution during the war. Poor or destitute families see their daughters as a form of trade for 'dowry' where payments in the form of cattle, gifts, and money are received from the intended husband. Cattle are poplar in the exchange of marriage transactions where teenage girls are exchanged for cattle, also men who are quite opulent get more wives and bears more children to strengthen their 'clan'.

Justice Bullen and other women's bodies committed their time and effort towards abolishing and eliminating forced and early child marriages to accomplish one of the Sustainable Development Goals. South Sudan cosponsored the 2013 and 2014 United Nations General Assembly resolutions on early, forced child marriage as well as the 2013 Human Rights Council resolution on early, forced child marriage. In the year 2014, South Sudan endorsed a joint statement at the Human Rights Council advocating for the resolution of child marriage. South Sudan consented to the Convention on the Rights of the Child in 2015 which sets a minimum age of marriage to 18, and the Convention on the Elimination of All Forms of Discrimination Against Women (CEDAW) in 2015, compelling all 10 states of South Sudan to ensure full consent to the marriage.

South Sudan is yet to sign or endorse the African Charter on the Rights and Welfare of the Child and Article 21 regarding the prohibition of Child Marriage. As of 2013, South Sudan signed but did not endorse the African Charter on Human and People's Rights on the Rights of Women in Africa including Article 6 hence setting the minimum age for marriage as 18 years of age. Moving forward, South Sudan is one of the countries championing the commitment to end child marriage under Ministerial Commitment on comprehensive sexuality education and sexual and reproductive health services for adolescents and young people in Eastern and Southern Africa. A move towards the positive, South Sudan supported endorsements to strengthen efforts to eliminate child marriage. The government emphasized that it is particularly complex in dealing with child marriage and preventing early dropouts of girls from schools in states such as Upper Nile. In the case of Upper Nile, most schools have been destroyed due to incessant conflicts and are yet to be rebuilt. As a nation, South Sudan's Ministry of Gender, Child and Social Welfare led the development of a Strategic National Action Plan (SNAP) 2017-2030. The development of the action plan was spearheaded by a National Task Force to End Child Marriage, and the National Gender-Based Violence Sub-Cluster and the Child Protection Sub-Cluster, with technical and financial support from UNICEF and UNFPA.

The development process also involved the Ministry of Health, Ministry of General Education and Instruction, and the Ministry of Justice, and many non-governmental stakeholders. Still, there is currently a lack of government leadership to execute the action plan. On the positive side, special protection units are established at a certain police station to make sure girls and women can freely and confidently report cases of gender-based violence. Despite enacting laws and establishing a response team in the police station, rebuilding quality schools in rural areas are important. Educating the girl child not only guarantees a better quality of life for the girl child but also put South Sudan in a state ready for positive change in its country reform particularly in its political and socio-economic development.

Protecting girl child is what Justice Bullen Panchol had been advocating for , to give quality education to girl child. This exemplary is evident in all his daughters today as they are all well-educated.

CHAPTER 9

SETTING UP TOUGH PREVENTIVE MEASURES AGAINST THE ABDUCTION OF CHILDREN BY CATTLE RUSTLERS IN JONGLEI STATE.

Nuer say that it is cattle that destroy people, for "more people have died for the sake of a cow than for any other cause."

—Evans-Pritchard, The Nuer (1940)

In Jonglei state, the issue of cattle raiding is not a new occurrence as it is a fact of life for most pastorals in the region, however, it became alarming as it gravely affected the most remote areas that are often less recorded in the news. It claimed the life and properties of hundreds of thousands. At the borders of South Sudan's Jonglei tribal line, the vicious cycles of laying siege and raiding Dinka Bor, Twi, Duk, Lou Nuer and Murle ethnic groups led to grave casualties and this continued on a relatively repetitive basis. More than six years of post-independence, a large number of South Sudanese states remained lawless. An example of this, is the Jonglei state where peace remained largely vague. In spite of the relentless efforts to put an end to the violence by the government of South Sudan, national organizations, international bodies, and even religious movements, all proved abortive.

Evidently, the systematic exploitations of customary cattle raiding acts and child abductions are largely influenced most of the cattle rustling conflicts exacerbated by the political leaders, however, the position of the intercommunity violence was vaguely part of mainstream dialogue proffering political solutions. In addition, as loyalty between political factions and pastoralist local militia fade away, the propagation of informal armed groups whose motivation is most times separate from primary agenda of opposition forces or state whose behalf they once laid down their lives presents increasing roadblocks to peacebuilding efforts. Abandoning native realities presents dire implications for the future of peace.

In South Sudan, Cattle is not just a herd of animal, it is considered as a symbol of affluence, it identifies the social class of South Sudanese indigenes and has also contributed largely to their local economy. As said by youth from Jonglei state "You cannot marry without cows… and you are not a man without cows". Asides differentiating social classes in a community, it creates an avenue for desperation and can be a major instigator for conflict. In Jonglei, there are three large ethnic groups or clan i.e. the Dinka, Nuer, and Murle people. The Dinka Bor people have the Northern Dinka and Southern Dinka. The complexity of cattle raiding among these three groups i.e. Dinka Bor, Nuer, and Murle of Jonglei state. Historically, the Greater Dinka Bor, Nuer, and Murle are indigenous pastoralists who value cattle and have a long history of joining in cattle rustling and child abduction according to McCallum and Okech, 2013.

Amongst these three communities, animals particularly cattle take a high place. Not only are livestock a source of livelihood, but they are also a major source of cultural and social pride. For years, centuries even, cattle have remained major support of the local economy among various communities in South Sudan. All through history, pastoral communities in Jonglei see cattle as a way of measuring social status and class, as well as a means of indicating wealth. Every so often, the possession of cattle plays a major role, especially in marriage or restoration of justice i.e. reparation. Ever since 2011, the world attention has been focused on building South Sudan's governing institutions. Therefore, the inherent issues such as castle raiding and child abduction have been left unattended to particularly in Jonglei state.

Natives of Jonglei state have and value culture, traditions, customs, and individual heritage, as well as other qualities that individually identify them as Greater Dinka Bor, Murle, and Nuer respectively. This means tribal identity is influential when it comes to how each ethnic group interact as a community. In addition, there is a general belief that ethnic connections among Dinka Bor, Murle, and Nuer have been impaired contributing to the growth in hatred amongst each ethnic tribe which reveals itself in form of child abduction and cattle rustling in Jonglei. There is also the general belief common among non-Dinkas in Jonglei state, particularly among Nuer and Murle natives that Dinka Bor led government administration is partial or despotic, marginality, monopolistic toward indigenes of Jonglei who are not from Dinka Bor. Women and children are abducted and slaughtered during raids as a consequence of refusing to oblige their captors. Also, properties such as local houses grass thatch or tukul made of wood and grass are often set ablaze and destroyed. In the same vein, rape cases were reported during these raids. Many youths acknowledge that violent raiding and child abductions are major contributors to death in Jonglei. For example, in 2013, a single raid in Dinka and Nuer accounted that over 10,000 herds of cattle were raided, and also the death of more than 2000 people, as well as hundreds of children, were abducted all in the space of three weeks.

The South Sudan government is quite aware of the socio-economic primacy of cattle and has traditionally taken initiative on animal health and protection. The army as well as the police are deployed during its dry season to prevent cattle rustling and community-based health professionals help with the administering of vaccines. However, it appears the conflict has taken superiority over the cattle. Hence, forcing the government to divert resources from livestock towards the war effort. The ineffectiveness of South Sudan's legal system with criminal cases i.e. prolonged hearing of criminal cases hence forcing people to take matters into their hands and enforcing justice the way they see fit (Manyok, 2017). This led to the development of informal armies in South Sudan, the absence of justice in the early days of attacks leaves room for revenge as the only alternative to justice available to South Sudanese natives.

White Army or "dec bor" are originally referred to groups of native Nuer pastoralists that came together to form a vigilante to protect their children from abduction and cattle against raids. Certain interpretations maintain that the White Army takes its name from the white ash younger herders cover themselves in to shield themselves against mosquito bites. However, the members of the White army clarified it is to differentiate between the Nuer raiders from the "Dec char" i.e. the Black Army as they insultingly refer to expert soldiers whom they disregard with disdain. In the course of the Second Sudanese Civil War, the decentralized aggregate of herders carrying weapons gathered for limited periods of time so as to fight, hence scattering back to cattle camps.

A slacking and shifting group rather than a standing force with a stable and defined organizational structure, the coalition of herders carrying weapons fighting under the guise of the name "White Army" has evolved all through the phases of the conflict in South Sudan. Sometimes less and more active with periods of remobilization calmness since the signing of the 2005 CPA. The White Army also has had a second occurrence playing a rather active role in the conflict. They are largely motivated by the killings of Nuer natives in Juba after conflict broke out between Dinka and Nuer natives of the elite presidential guard on Dec 15, 2013. Nowadays, the White Army mentions groups of armed youthful Eastern Nuer, distinguish from the formal SPLA-IO ranks, however without who the SPLM-IO would have fixed credible military force.

In the bid to incorporate peace-making efforts, opinions from youths in rural and urban areas of Jonglei state living under opposition and government control. The frustrations of youth are apparent in that they perceive the need for their participation in peacebuilding, but lack the capacity, and in many cases the education, and resources to take action. Jonglei state youths recognize the need to communicate with each other and to set up platforms that are not affiliated politically but based on a common desire to achieve peace, at all levels of society and political life. Lots of youth challenge the domination of political leaders and their cruel manipulation of communities and youth in support of their selfish agendas. Several political leaders act in personal or factional interest, and not in the interests of peace, nation-building nor the development of their communities. The youth recognize their own contributions to violent conflict, including cattle rustling to amass wealth, to pay dowries, and take vengeance for abuses of their kin, especially of women. They mentioned that the reduction of cattle rustling entails increased security, more and effective policing, and a drastic reduction in corruption. Essentially expressed by both female and male informants, changes in the attitudes and cultural norms that determine marriage processes and the roles of women are required. Youth, by cultural definition, are seeking adulthood through "forming close relationships outside the family, often resulting in marriage and children" – to use one of the indicators of adulthood proposed by the World Bank.

For women, there is a little or no youthful phase as they tend to be married off at a young age and socially, once this happens, they are not referred to as youth anymore. If young women are to play vital roles in the role of peacebuilding as part of South Sudan's youth, their literacy, social skill development needs to be improved in accordance with the release from social pressures to marry for dowry needs. These changes are essential for female and male youth and are displayed in different forms. Some youths could describe dialogue and negotiation they engaged in implanting peace talks. These encompassed the development of non-politicized platforms and youth forums that they can use to pull strings for the recognition of their needs, rights, and opportunities to engage meaningfully in peacemaking processes. Youth identified the need to build understanding and cooperation between ethnic groups who traditionally and currently take sides against each other. This can be achieved through the setting up of non-controversial sporting, and other activity centres and exchange visits across ethnicities. Frequently both young women and men sought resources to lift them from poverty and reliance on illegal and/or immoral activities, or political patronage, for their survival and livelihoods. Only when freed from these constraints, and with adequate resources, do they believe they will usefully express themselves individually and collectively in the search for peace, and the prosperity of their country and communities.

One of the biggest hindrances to justice accountability in Jonglei state is the radical weakness of its criminal justice system, especially when taking into account the gravity and scale of the crimes connected with inner-communal violence. A requirement for directing accountability will, therefore, be effective measures to strengthen justice, police, and prison institution in Jonglei state. The official footprint of the justice system in Jonglei's 11 counties is ruthlessly limited particularly when considering the geographic size and population coverage which is an estimate of 1.3 million. The presence of the judicial system in Jonglei is limited to two High Court judges and two Magistrate Court judges, and eight prosecutors in Bor town, etc. Additionally, the official system seriously lacking capacities, skills, and knowledge. This appears to be the case for most judges, police, prosecutors, and defence counsel. There is also a shortage of access to legal tools, copies of laws in force, as well as a corresponding comprehension of its application. There is minute administrative support and much of the infrastructure is dilapidated. Lots of the officers in the police force are illiterate who lack basic skills to undertake primary criminal investigations and maintain investigation records.

Even though the South Sudan Police Service is deployed in each Payam of all counties in Jonglei, its personnel are not trained nor are they fully resourced to respond to certain challenges which they encounter on a day-to-day basis. In areas close to Bor County, the seat of the state capital, police stations lack proper and basic communication resources. In Jonglei state, even in South Sudan as a whole, the customary justice processes feature prominently within the justice system. The usual or traditional justice is closely related to the formal system through the practice and Transitional Constitution of the Republic of South Sudan (TCSS). These practices are basically reconciliatory with a focus on properties such as land, determining compensation in property, and adultery cases. Although not fully equipped with legal and skill authorities, several customary processes settle in serious criminal cases as well as many 'authorize' the detention of persons in County and State prisons. A number of 'Special Courts' of customary chiefs have been established to arbitrate inter-communal violence, even though not on the level discovered in Jonglei. These processes should be incorporated into a justice strategy for inter-communal violence in Jonglei state, however, be harmonized as far as possible with basic human rights norms.

CHAPTER TEN
CONTROL NOMADIC RANGING: INTRODUCING PROHIBITIVE LAWS TO CATTLE RUSTLERS.

Historically, South Sudanese are herders and farmers. Cattle are a cultural and agricultural backbone for several nomadic pastoralists in Africa. The influence of livestock theft on marginalized community is austere. It denies people of their livelihood and increasing the high rate of poverty. Oftentimes during castle raiding, breadwinners of the family are injured or killed during rustling, fuelling common criticisms and revenge attacks. The cross-border criminal networks make use of advanced logistics and market information to carry on their illicit activities. Cattle raiding as a type of organized crime is rooted in the wider cattle trade business permitted by government corruption, with state officials turning a blind eye or teaming up with criminals. Certain politicians make use of bribery to persuade rural communities to get involved in cattle raising networks. The purpose is two-fold: to solicit for money to fund increasingly expensive campaigns for power overstaying, as well as to attack, disenfranchise, and disempower citizens favourable to their rivals.

Cattle raiders also exploit weal cross-border coordination between governments in the region. Cattle owners recruit and arm rural warriors to rob cattle for sale to abattoirs in towns or cross into neighbouring countries like Ethiopia, Uganda and Kenya where they sell cattle commercially. Stolen cattle are easy to move about as they can be camouflaged as a legal commodity. Other East African countries response to the issue of cattle raiding has been ineffective. South Sudanese states in the region have for years responded to cattle raiding inaction, ineffective disarmament resourcefulness, or indiscriminate force. An important step that has not been delivered on its potential is the endorsing of the 2008 Protocol on the Prevention, Combating, and Elimination of Cattle Raiding in Eastern Africa.

The protocol aims to address cattle raiding by improving regional collaboration, harmonizing legislation, as well as the adoption of livestock identification records and systems. On the other, this has not been implemented due to Uganda being the country left of 13 member states of Eastern Africa Police Chiefs Cooperation Organization (EAPCCO) that has endorsed the practice. This practice or protocol can give a region a common legal framework or policy to handle crisis. The lack of support from East African states that makes most governments in the region not to take the issue of cattle raiding as a heinous crime.

In several East African countries, there is no law that necessitates the source of cattle slaughterhouses be noticed. The nonexistence of anti-stock theft police units in certain areas of the countries makes communities particularly rural communities vulnerable to armed raiders. Their susceptibility is heightened as a result of the areas affected by cattle raiding the most are categorized by underdeveloped, under-resourced security structures and an inadequate government presence. Justice Bullen Panchol took this movement to heart and put in intense effort in making the government commit to put an end to senseless revenge killings and destructions of marginalized pastoralists. This should involve sanctioning the Eastern Africa Police Chiefs Cooperation Organization (EAPCCO) protocol and offering better legal basis for the regulation of registration trade for livestock. With the combination of technological inventions and better controls, the protocol's legal basis for regulating trade of livestock is expected to be strengthened. Controlling the market also has the potential of ensuring true pastoralists profit from cattle rather than via partnering with corrupt criminal cartels. In the instance where East Africa fail to acclimatize to the threat, cattle raiding may spread into new areas and create another organized criminal armed pastoralist.

Justice Bullen Panchol Awal stressed that, the criminalization of cattle rustling by the law-enacting body in South Sudan is a welcome development, however, the issue is that the criminalizing of this criminal act will move the attention of potential perpetrators to other types of crime. It is also equally possible that it will to certain extent discourage the altogether. This extent should therefore be considered together with involvements of all government stakeholders. Implementing laws can facilitate technological strategies such as electronic branding as well as online registration. Governments should have total control over livestock markets where livestock permits issued by the states are exchanged between buyers and sellers the same method motorists exchange logbooks when a vehicle change ownership. This method will simplify taxation. Cooperation of cross-border between countries in East Africa should improve the existing common objective of a regional response to the transnational nature of cattle raiding. This calls for consolidation of the current structure of the legislature as well as for the increased security cooperation amongst the South Sudanese state in that region. Also, this calls for the immediate need to re-define the problem as a cross-country crime following by the sanctioning of a united legal structure to prevent perpetrators from looking for refuge in any countries in the region. Additional policy research to notify the execution of prospective measures. The design and execution of policies should be steered by informed research rather than by politics. This will make sure programs are taking into account the aspirations and expectations of the intended communities. The participation of affected communities towards looking for permanent solution towards finding a long-lasting solution to issues. Local solutions such as locally consensual disarmament principle should be formed across all stages. In cases where forceful disarmament is not following intended productive goal, more sustainable measures should be considered especially development projects that meets rural residence needs.

CHAPTER ELEVEN
BRING LAW AND ORDER TO THE GRASSROOTS: RURAL VILLAGES.

During war outbreaks, all country, urban, and rural areas suffer from the chaos and dystopia, however, when dialogue and cease-fire are in the works, it takes extra effort and enforcement to put an all-time stop to war in the grassroots particularly the rural areas. Factors primarily being illiteracy, these people are easily swayed to conflict and also at the receiving end due to lack of proper prompt communication resources as well as prompt response infrastructure such as fully equipped hospitals. The quest to bringing law and order to the rural areas is sure to be quite effort, resources, and time intensive. In 2013, South Sudan succession into civil war just two years after independence leaving communities, families, institutions, especially judicial institutions in a state of devastation.

Being extremely vulnerable as a result of years of war against Khartoum, certain institutions are yet to infiltrate all through the territory, although some were in the process of formation. Areas that are far beyond the claim of the state were still not left ungoverned. Customary chiefs and the rich fibre of tribal rules and norms applied to settle disputes have played important role in uniting communities together and strengthening the fibre of communities. Although this was popularly applied during the years of the North and South opposing each other in the Sudanese Civil War, in spite of the numerous challenges they face. The new country South Sudan encountered a hard time with the militarization of public and private life, personalized, and impunity rule. As a result, constitutionalism and the rule of law are the twin pillars of a state governed by law have suffered. This begs the question; how can the rule of law and the judiciary help to establish strength and stability in South

Sudan? Also, what roles does the judicial system i.e. the customary courts that make up the lower rings of the official justice system contribute to this initiative?

In the case of the ownership of unlicensed gun culture by the average South Sudanese and the Absence of rule of law stretches the role of the military in an apparently democratic and civilian-governed South Sudan. The current state of affairs in South Sudan shows the embarrassingly lowest level of the rule of law that operates in South Sudan. The rule of law denotes a state in which all, leaving nothing as an exception are answerable to the law. The law and other institutions established rules and procedures. Right from inception, South Sudan has had a rule of law problems. Particularly, it has been described by weak institutions even the judiciary, which is submissive to the executive arm of government, personalized power, lack of trust institution (not leaving out the judiciary), culture violence, military interference on public life as well as in the administration of justice and settling of disputes.

According to its 2013 formative report, South Sudan's judiciary i.e. the ICJ – International Commission of Jurists condemned the obvious weakness of South Sudan's rule of law. It pictures this report with the case of SPLA General who was charged with a lawsuit at the High Court in Juba who "visited the sitting judge" accompanied by armed men and demanded to know when the verdict will be ready. Although this shows an extreme case of power intimidation of a judicial officer, it is also suggestive of other actions that bargains the independence of the judiciary. Similarly, the capacity limitations of the formal judiciary to which the short supply of judges, insufficient number of courts over a vast county or territory, as well as poor working conditions for most judicial officers, hence restricting the reach of legal institutions in the new state. The report later revealed that a huge number of cases that reach the courts are decided by the underrated, yet serious customary courts staffed by customary chiefs.

The influence of customary courts created under the Local Government Act of 2009 states that customary court are only limited to "customary disputes. During the practice, they listen and decide a wide range of cases that comprises of assault, rape, theft, homicide, etc. primarily because the customary courts are often the most preferred courts by litigants than statutory courts.

While in the bush and in the early days of law profession, Justice Bullen Panchol was a judge to some of the customary court in his early years of practice before retiring to the bush, the military way. In atypical customary court, they are faced with overwhelming number of cases and are decided by critical customary courts chiefs. These courts fill a major gap in provision of legal litigation and arbitral services left by formal justice that have potential to be critical towards the security in local areas and towns in South Sudan.

Despite the role of customary courts in play in the delivery of justice and delivery of security for citizens, hence vital institutions have encountered strains due to prolonged duration of war. Not leaving out the intimidation by the military that were in charge of liberated areas and the weakening of the influence and authority of community leaders of returning exiles whose traditions and views have been transformed by past experiences. The Customary courts in South Sudan also limited by being placed within local government administration, which is widely known as ineffective and provides little effort.

On some occasions, Chiefs find it hard to enforce their decisions and in certain cases been openly condemned and threatened with physical violence. Traditional leaders are restricted in terms of bigger conflict cases between communities relating to access to livestock pasture and water. The increase of ownership of arms within the general population in South Sudan adds another layer of exertion. Due to the lack of proper police presence in rural areas, the customary courts are ruled by chiefs and often depend on SPLA to fit into the enforcing of law and order roles to supply security as well as implement customary court decisions.

Oftentimes, the SPLA fail to fill in this capacity but instead act with freedom, hence leaving the citizen without security and option when they encounter violations. This reduces the respect of law and order in South Sudan, this further compromise and complicate the work of customary chiefs and increasing the level of insecurity in prevailing local areas. Although customary courts remain incompetent in several ways, in their absence then lawlessness will be the order of the day in most territories. In fact, the most important rile that these traditional institutions play in the delivery of arbitral services during the conflicts post-independence has been recognised by the United Nations which has created "conflict resolution committees" in camps for internally displaced people.

In the bid to intervene in the state of rule of law interventions, other than teaching the small number of available judges, prosecutors, and magistrates who were placed in the post-CPA period, the justice sector suffers from an acute shortage of judicial officers and prosecutors. Besides, the main hire of new judges in 2013 was close to the start of the beginning of the post-independence civil war and no notably improved delivery in service has been carried out. The lack of infrastructure of the justice sector with few and dilapidating facilities that exist are what is available in Juba.

During the post-independence era, the support given to the customary courts took the practice of training by the United Nations Mission in South Sudan as well as other partners. Circumstantial evidences opine that interventions may or may not have had an apparent impact due to several structural factors including low literacy level, heterogeneity of customary norms, and accustomed practices that may victimize women and youth in a diverse South Sudan suffering from complex insecurity. The UNDP i.e.

United Nations Development Program's attempt to harmonize customary laws is done at a dawdling pace, but later got interrupted by the incessant conflict. The referral of cases between customary courts and the limited available magistrate courts that should perform a supervisory role over the former is quite awkward.

High Court introduced on trial basis by Chief Justice in two regions improved the delivery of judicial services, however, they were not adequately funded. The inadequate backing for customary courts shows the mistreatment of local and state governments in relation to national government institutions. Doing this led to multiple effects such as increasing the potency of local conflicts, missed opportunity to build a culture of the rule of law from the grassroots villages leaving the periphery mostly ungoverned. Therefore, this contributed to the entrenchment and use of force as well as insecurity prompting citizen to embrace violence as an alternative to resolve disputes.

Proposed Recommendation

Rule of law is essential to the future and stability of South Sudan. Even though the rule of law will be formed by a much broader political context in South Sudan hence spreading the reach of informal courts into the ungoverned areas of South Sudan is an essential in stabilising the country. Increasing the access to 3-4 week-long fundamental training for paralegals to guide the customary court chiefs on legal cases. Additionally, in consolidating the legal state of these courts, increasing the use of paralegals who are closest to the rural areas and understand the dynamics of the cause of conflict. Also, it provides additional opportunities for women and youth to participate and represent their community in their capacity and behalf of their peers.

Establish a national structure e.g. harmonization law based on the constitution of criminal laws and human rights. This would establish a homogeneity in terms of how the customary courts function and arrange for opportunities for the sharing of experiences amongst the customary law panels from other parts of the country. The national structure must detach the customary courts from the underfunded arm of government i.e. the local government and bring them within national judiciary. Doing this would respond to the relegation of the customary courts, confirm its critical role in the delivery of justice and safety for citizens, improve oversights over them by magistrates and judges, as well as build their capacity by providing resources, including token remuneration for decision-makers i.e. panel of judges.

In accordance to the Local Government Act of South Sudan, customary courts lack the jurisdiction over criminal matters except in the case related to a 'customary interface'. Even though the word "customary interface" is not recognised by law, it is presumably referring to criminal offences related with the issues like adultery, cattle rustling, children abduction, which mostly the kind of cases handled by the traditional chiefs. In spite of the jurisdictional restraint, the customary courts usually hear a lot of criminal disputes and have the power to sanction a number of criminal punishments e.g. corporal punishments, fines, and prison sentences. In certain areas, customary courts even judge complex crime such as rape or murder. One of the common solutions provided in instances of murder is the culprit to be mandated to pay a certain number of cattle to the family of the deceased to compensate them for their loss. The number of cattle that has to be remitted varies from community to community as well as the nature of the killing. However, such solutions offer a significant means of handling conflict in areas where official state institutions do not exist.

The Passing of Judge Bullen Panchol Awal: Family and Individual Reflections:

Eng. John Deng Diar Diing's Reflection – Mombasa, Kenya

Father, Justice Bullen Panchol Awal Alier

You have been a father and role model to me in close proximity for fairly five short but productive years. You were and still are, in your grave an epitome of inspiration and a beacon of what knowledge means to a generation and generations thereafter.

As a young ambitious schoolboy, I looked out for role models in our society to anchor my academic goal posts on. Your name sprung out in every discussion as an astute, gifted and upright intellectual leader of your generation. Indeed, you embodied nobility and graciousness in education.

Your ingenuity, honesty, modesty and strong belief in truthful and just society had always cut you out. Your academic silhouette guided many young girls and boys to their academic destination in Refugee Camps and beyond during the difficult times of war.

But not until you became a father to me and grandfather to my children when our intellectual interaction took a practical tutelage.

Our conversation had always taken five minutes of greetings and exchange of pleasantries but was immediately followed by what was, is and will be good for our society. Your encouragement of me to always look out for my likeminded age mates to focus on matters that unite and guide our people to a secure tomorrow has always kept me in contemplation. It is my hope, I will make good use of your inspiration for the betterment of our people someday.

Your objectivity and wisdom will be missed by us, your family, community and our country. Our community in particular needs moral guidance when their unity is on trial. They needed you now as a leader and an elder.

Even as we talked that afternoon on your way to the hospital, I was still hopeful that your book which we had discussed would be our next topic and your recovery. Little did I know that you would be no more in 28 hours. It was heart wrenching and antagonizing to bear the pain of your loss the whole night to break it to my dear wife in the morning. It was and still is a complete devastation!

In the hindsight, you left as a proud father, with well-educated children and promising grandchildren. You have lived a purposeful life. A life that a man of your personality deserves. Although it was our prayer that God kept you to reap your investment, we had no more power than power of medics and wish of God.

As they say, we only wish but God decides. He decided to take you when we needed you around longer. Unfortunately, it is only Him that controls longevity of Life. He decided to take you on the 13/05/2020.

As I bid you this farewell, I want you to know that I am proud that I share heritage with you in my children and that I look forward to the reincarnation of your greatness in my little boys and a daughter.

My God rest your soul in Peace, Baba.

Susan Bullen Panchol Awal's Reflection – Mombasa, Kenya

Dad, Bullen Panchol Awal Alier Gaar,

As we look back over time, we find ourselves wondering …… did we remember to thank you enough for all you have done for us?

For all the times you were by our sides to help and support us, to celebrate our successes, to understand our problems and accept our defeats or for teaching us by your example the value of hard work, good judgment, courage and integrity.

We wonder if we ever thanked you for the sacrifices you made to let us have the very best. If we have forgotten to show our gratitude enough for all the things you did,

we are thanking you now. And we are hoping you knew all along, how much you meant to Us Daddy.

You were the best dad anyone could ever ask for, am grateful to God Almighty for letting me be born by a great Man like you; Justice Bullen Panchol Awal.

Rest well baba till we meet again.

To our Martin Alier,

You were an angel on earth my beloved brother. I know the world was not fair to you, but you have always tried your best,

you were full of life, always laughing and smiling with a kind and beautiful heart. You were a man of the people always standing up for what is right,

your level of intelligence was beyond.

You may not be with us physically, but you will always be in our hearts, we will always remember all the memories we shared together.

May you find the perfect peace that the earth denied you; my beloved brother till we meet again.

By Susan Nyiel Bullen Panchol.

Asara Bullen Panchol Awal's Reflection – Juba, South Sudan

People don't choose to which family they should be born in, but I would choose to be your daughter again. You are the best father anyone would have wished for. Growing up under your wings as both a mother and father figure, mentor and inspiration, I aspire to be you. Through you, I have learned that qualities like honesty, integrity, just and hard work are what makes a quality admirable life. I know I never got the chance to tell you that you are my Hero and I am sad about that but I will not remember you in sadness, I will not remember you in tears, I will remember you through a woman of dignity you were raising. I know you can read through my heart and I also know you are with me every minute, so I want to promise you that your admirable legacy is alive and will always be alive to the world. Rest in Glory Dad because you served humanity with dignity and you achieved your purpose on this earth. Until we meet again!

Nyiel Bullen Panchol Awal (Toto)'s Reflection – Montreal, Canada

Dear Daddy! You had dedicated your life to us, your children until your very last breath, we might never have told you how proud we are to call you our dad, but you will always be one in a million. God makes us what we are, but I'll say he used your amazing fatherly aspects to make me so much of who I am today. Your positive outlook, your passion for us and your drive to do things in the most fair and just way are what I am emulating to achieve. Thank you for being such a hero, may your soul continue to rest in peace. we love you but God loved you the most.

And to my dear brother Martin Alier, you were such a sweet soul that got along with everyone, although death robbed you from us at an early age, we will forever cherish the moments we lived together and called you a brother. We were lucky to have you as part of us you might be gone from our sights, but you will always be in our hearts.

Rest in eternal peace brother, we loved you but Almighty loves you more. by Toto Nyiel.

Diing Bullen Panchol Awal's Reflection – Juba, South Sudan

A loving person who gave us all his love, care and a surname passed on 13/05/2020, our dad was a firm believer. he was a best friend to anyone in need. Our dad had a very simple way of life, he believed that you just don't get anything for nothing everything has to be earned through hard-work, persistence and honesty. Our dad was our hero, he was the most courageous and resourceful man, we never questioned if he loved or cared for us because he made it so obvious. We'll always remember that caring heart that you gave us because there will be no one to replace you in our hearts.

RIP DAD.

Kut Bullen Panchol Awal's Reflection – Nairobi, Kenya

Even though the way we mourn a loss may be different in certain cultures, it's something that we must all learn to accept if we want to heal...your memories will forever live in me.

REST IN PEACE DAD.

Ayen Bullen Panchol Awal (Dolly)'s Reflection – Mombasa, Kenya

Daddy dear,

When I think of you, all that comes to my mind are good memories. Throughout your lifetime, you taught us integrity, honesty, and hard work. If I were given a thousand chances, I would choose you as my dad over and over again. You were both a father and a mother to me. Throughout you dedicated your life to ensure that we have a good life. You're my hero, my daily inspiration. Every day I wake up thanking God for giving me a daddy like you. You were not only a father or a brother or uncle or friend to people, you were a legend, a hero to everyone. Your passion and infectious energy towards everyone were always so admirable. May your soul continue resting in peace? We love you so much, but God loves you more.

Dear Brother Martin,

You were such a kind and loving brother anyone would ever wish to have.it was too early and unexpected for you to leave us but its beyond human comprehension. We believe that everything happens for a reason and in God's own time. We will always remember and cherished the time you were with us, the moments we laughed and cried together. You will forever be in our hearts, rest in eternal peace. We love you so much, but God loves you more.

Dr. Luka Biong Deng Kuol's Reflection – Boston, United States

Justice Bullen Panchol:

South Sudan has lost one of its refined and seasoned lawyers, Justice Bullen Panchol, member of the Supreme Court of South Sudan. I came to know Justice Panchol when Dr John Garang appointed us in 1991 to the legal and constitutional committee to draft and review basic laws for the New Sudan to be presented to the SPLM National Convention in 1994. The committee was chaired by Commander Ayuen Alier (the current Director of the DDR Commission) and I was the only economist on the committee. During our deliberations over various laws, Justice Panchol exhibited rare traits of professionalism, integrity, humility and nobility. We became friends since then and I worked closely with him when he was a member of national constitutional court in Khartoum, a duty that he performed with distinction. One of his closest friends remembered him as one of the few elders who would like to be associated with his mother, as he would always introduce himself in social gatherings as Panchol Abeny. Justice Panchol would be remembered as freedom fighter, martyr and one of the founders of legal system for South Sudan. My condolences to his family and relatives. May Almighty God Rest His Soul in Eternal Peace.

Majeep Ayuen Kou's Reflection – Juba, South Sudan

Tears can't stop flowing after this family tragedy. In your loving memory Martin, I promise to always love you as we have always been from childhood. Your absence in this World will not mean your absent in my life. You are and will always be a true brother. To Justice Bullen Panchol Children.

I feel your pains losing two people in a family within days a part. Mzee Justice Bullen Panchol deserves what a gallant citizen deserves from his country but unfortunately that has not been forthcoming and does not make him less patriotic. Each one of us who know this noble family will grieve with you to give Mzee and Martin a respectful goodbye.

May your souls rest in peace.

Ajak Deng Chiengkou's Reflection – Melbourne, Australia

As the immediate and extended members of Pan Awal Alier, I know what you are going through. It is hard for anyone to bear. Losing Panchol then followed by Alier is another pain, but you all have to be strings. I know it will be hard for children because all were closer to their dad and brother. There is no way one can bring you together to give you the message of support. I am praying that all of you find the emotional support that you need these times. I was not able to tag Asara, Marina and Avena and the rest of children on Facebook.

Ambassador Maluk Mach Tiir's Reflection – Juba, South Sudan

Justice Panchol Abeny since childhood was a genius brain with a lot in common from his father and mother. He adapted his eloquent straightforwardness, braveness & intelligence from Awal Alier and adapted his bold objective in communication, hardworking and argumentative intelligent from his mother Abeny Tiir. This is apparently our rare traits in our genes. The only person who was close friend to Awal Alier was, Aluong Kang from Bor, those two were known as highly intelligent. In most schools Justice

Panchol went to, he was always known as active in leadership roles serving in student unions and student councils.

Samuel Ajak Thiong's Reflection – Juba, South Sudan

Death is sad enough when anticipated, but even worse when unexpected.

But no death is as hard on the living as the unexpected death of our Uncle Bullen Panchol Awal Alier. His death is a sad loss to Pan Ang'akuei, Bor Community and the nation.

It's a tragic and unexpected loss. I am still in disbelief. I don't think the reality has hit me just yet. Our community has lost an elder, a father and a legal expert. I know how difficult this loss touches all people related to the Late Uncle Bullen. For most of us who lived in Juba with late Uncle Bullen Panchol, we have known him as both a cheerful and engaging personality, as well as a savvy and successful Supreme Court Judge. Late Bullen Panchol Awal had been involved in numerous high-profile cases before and during the liberation struggle and also during 6 years of CPA.

May his soul rest in eternal peace, I firmly believe that God will accept him with open arms for all the good he has done while he was with us serving the people of South Sudan.

Malith Ayiu's Reflection – Sydney, Australia

Today's not like other days; Pan Angakuei, Pan Bor and indeed the Republic of South Sudan has loss a judge, a leader, and the tower of intellect in justice Bullen Panchol Awal Alier. Justice Panchol was and will always remain, remembered as the fair judge, conservative by nature and a truths teller.

Judge, you left us peaceful memories as we mourn you. your love for your family and your community will remain as the guiding light of our future. We were fortunate to have you amongst us as the brother, uncle and indeed the father/grandpa to the next generations pan Awal Alier. Though we cannot see you at the moment you will always remain on our sides. Pan Angakuei will missed you. Rest In Peace Judge Bullen.

Mayom Deng Kwai's Reflection – Melboune, Australia

It is too hard to believe these double tragedies of Justice Bullen Panchol Awal Alier & his son Alier Panchol in just pace of two days only! This is doom! Late Panchol Awal Alier noted devastated by passing of his childhood, schoolmate, brother in law & best friend Prof Aggrey Ayuen Majok. The same things consequently happened to Alier his son as death of Alier's dad took devastating tolls on him which ended his life earlier. The saddest times ever! May the orphans withstand these overwhelming states!

Akol Aguek Ngong's Reflection – Vermont, United State

What a loss to Angakuei, Pan Bor, South Sudan, and global legal community! Uncle Justice Panchol Awal Alier was the epitome of the rule of law and justice for all: smart, intelligent, personable, and with wherewithal to speak to power on behalf of the downtrodden and voiceless. With legal education from both prestigious Khartoum University, Germany and UK, he was one of the brightest legal minds during liberation struggle and in South Sudan Government.

I briefly met Justice Panchol at their usual afternoon hang-out site (known as Tim Achiek Ngeth Angoh) near Konykonyo Market in Juba in February 2017. Justice Panchol was hanging out with Ustaz Maker Thiong Maal, Gen. Manyang Agok Aliet, Uncle Gen. Gaar Yuang Bior Gaar, Uncle Mangok Ajang Bol, Hon. Achiek Ngeth Angoh, and many other Bor elders. Justice Panchol's personability blew me away: firm handshake, eye contact, and genuine interest in knowing this young man on a brief visit to South Sudan from USA. He reminded me of their heyday encounters with my dad in Juba in mid 1980s sharing with elders how my dad would have been a great intellectual had he been given a chance to acquire a formal education.

During that chat, Justice Panchol called the elders' attention to our education, intellectualism, and access to global corridors of power conceding that their generation never had such education and access to where global power brokers make life and death decisions and wished we had been invited back to South Sudan and given opportunities to thrive and deliver for the new country. As he was leaving for some government meeting at the urging of his personal driver to get going to be on time, he pulled me aside and asked me to deliver his personal greetings to my dad, Aguek Ngong Kur, which I did a day later after I flew to Bor, South Sudan.

All I can say is I hope Justice Panchol has a book out there which I will have to order, read, and add to my book collections at my study, and if not, then this is a huge tragedy for generations to come. That level of intellect is rare to come by. Condolences to the family of Awal Alier, Wut Angakuei, Pan Bor, South Sudan, and global community for losing such a legal mind at a time South Sudan needs his legal contributions as it ponders on the way forward! May Almighty God rest his soul in eternal peace.

By Emanuel A. Chol's Reflection – Juba, South Sudan

Martin Alier was a gentleman, caring, patriotic, genius and above all man of people both young and old, a guy who doesn't minced his words. Very deeply saddens by his demised to the point I can't even imagine him missing among us. May his precious soul Rest In Peace

CONCLUSION

The late Justice Bullen Panchol did live his life for himself, his family, and particularly for the freedom and development of South Sudan. With his niche being the judicial arm of government, he made significant impact and sacrifices for the judicial system of South Sudan in a number of ways. From the Interim Constitution to his achievements in bringing awareness to the end of child marriage, bringing law and order to the grassroots via Customary Courts, etc. As we have flipped through the life of the no-nonsense judge, one of his final wishes before passing away was for the judiciary to gain its independence without interference from the Presidency as well as filtering the space-filling and corrupt judges leaving the judicial system in a rut.

This book is also about hope and reawakening the belief of a better South Sudan free from injustice, corruption, poverty, and nepotism. If not anything, this book hopes to re-instil the spirit of a freedom fighter for a just cause, in the same way, Justice Bullen would have or even better. For Justice Bullen Panchol Awal Alier, the ascension to heaven of a perfect judicial judge without any blemish starts with the willingness to be selfless, putting one's country first, and making the South Sudan constitution and Judicial system be one other African countries try to emulate.

GALLERY

Justice Bullen Panchol Awal Alier with Mading Ngor, January 2020

Young Bullen Panchol Awal Alier

Judge Bullen at John Hopkins University – Credit to Mario Makol

Judge Bullen's Interview with Dolku Media – Credit to Mading Ngor Akec Kuai Jan, 2020, Juba.

Justice Bullen Panchol Awal Alier taking a picture with Abraham Lincoln's Monument in Washington DC 2013.

The Fallen Distinguished Judge: The Constitutional Laws Fundamentalist

Cheerful Martin 'Marto' Alier Panchol Awal

Justice Bullen's 10 beautiful daughters.

The Fallen Distinguished Judge: The Constitutional Laws Fundamentalist

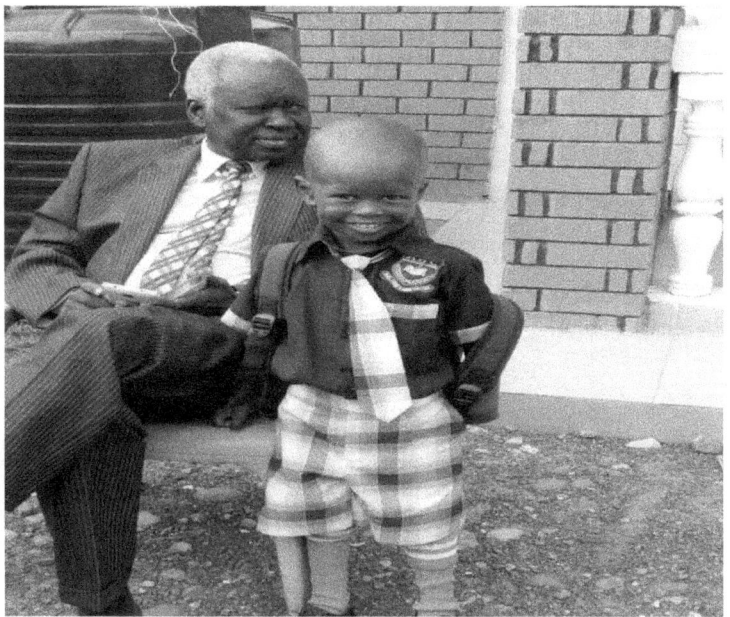

Justice Bullen and one of his grandchildren.

Ayuen Bullen Panchol Awal

The Fallen Distinguished Judge: The Constitutional Laws Fundamentalist

May 16th, 2020, the Funeral Service of Judge Bullen Panchol Awal Alier

Late Martin 'Marto' Bullen Panchol Alier, you will be missed.

Rest Well Our Icons top lawyers – All Fallen in 2020.

ABOUT THE AUTHOR

Majok Wutchok is Judge Bullen Panchol Awal's nephew. He grew up with Judge Bullen's children. Majok is highly skilful professional and well acclaimed proficient writer, technical website developer, publisher, blogger, motivational speaker, public health advocate, public health senior researcher and jack of all professional trades. He like spending most of his free time writing and publishing.

For any comment or support, contact Majok on admin@borpublishers.com

www.ingramcontent.com/pod-product-compliance
Lightning Source LLC
Chambersburg PA
CBHW070552050426
42450CB00011B/2826